Tax Guide 102

DEDUCTING JOB EXPENSES

by

Holmes F. Crouch
Tax Specialist

Published by

Allyear Tax Guides

20484 Glen Brae Drive
Saratoga, CA 95070

Copyright © 1998 by Holmes F. Crouch
All Rights Reserved

This book may not be reproduced in whole or part, by photocopying or any other means, without the express written permission of the author. Furthermore, this book is sold with the express understanding that the author is not engaged in rendering legal, accounting, or other professional service. The only warranty made is your money back on the cost of purchasing this book.

ISBN 0-944817-42-4

LCCN 97-75163

Printed in U.S.A.

Series 100
Individuals & Families

Tax Guide 102

DEDUCTING JOB EXPENSES

For other titles in print, see page 224.

The author: **Holmes F. Crouch**
For more about the author, see page 221.

PREFACE

If you are a knowledge-seeking **taxpayer** looking for information, this book can be helpful to you. It is designed to be read — from cover to cover — in less than eight hours. Or, it can be "skim-read" in about 30 minutes.

Either way, you are treated to **tax knowledge . . . *beyond the ordinary*.** The "beyond" is that which cannot be found in IRS publications, FedWorld on-line services, tax software programs, or on CD-ROMs.

Taxpayers have different levels of interest in a selected subject. For this reason, this book starts with introductory fundamentals and progresses onward. You can verify the progression by chapter and section in the table of contents. In the text, "applicable law" is quoted in pertinent part. Key phrases and key tax forms are emphasized. Real-life examples are given . . . in down-to-earth style.

This book has 12 chapters. This number provides depth without cross-subject rambling. Each chapter starts with a head summary of meaningful information.

To aid in your skim-reading, informative diagrams and tables are placed strategically throughout the text. By leafing through page by page, reading the summaries and section headings, and glancing at the diagrams and tables, you can get a good handle on the matters covered.

Effort has been made to update and incorporate all of the latest tax law changes that are *significant* to the title subject. However, "beyond the ordinary" does not encompass every conceivable variant of fact and law that might give rise to protracted dispute and litigation. Consequently, if a particular statement or paragraph is crucial to your own specific case, you are urged to seek professional counseling. Otherwise, the information presented is general and is designed for a broad range of reader interests.

The Author

INTRODUCTION

If you are an **employee,** and you incur "job expenses" on behalf of your profession and/or your employer, you are entitled to certain tax deductions for your expenditures. The rationale for this deductibility is: *cost of earning income.*

The cost of earning income is a long-standing tax principle of entrepreneurial man. You spend money to earn money, after which you are taxed on your net earnings. You are income taxed, social security taxed, medicare taxed, and — in some cases — alternative minimum taxed.

If you want to pay less tax, file Form 1040 and attach to it **Form 2106:** *Employee Business Expenses.* This, potentially, could be the most important deduction form on your return. Not all eligible employees know about it. Many of those who do know about it shun it, because of the homework, recordkeeping, and limitations involved. Yet, it is a very valuable form that can serve you well, if you are willing to familiarize yourself with its rules and procedures. What we are trying to do in this book is to encourage you to use Form 2106, where applicable, and not be deterred from it by the "disallowance jungle" created by the IRS.

What has happened over the years is that Congress — and the IRS — have gone out of their way to discourage employees from claiming their rightful deductions. The biggest discouragement hurdle in this regard is *The 2% AGI Rule.* (The acronym AGI stands for Adjusted Gross Income.) In a nutshell, this rule says that all job-related expenses must exceed 2% of your AGI before they are tax recognized. The irony is that if you file a joint return with your spouse (who may not incur job expenses), your spouse's income increases the 2% hurdle before any deduction is allowable.

Your basic right to a tax deduction for job expenses is set forth straightforwardly in Section 162(a) of the Internal Revenue Code. The preamble to this section reads in part as—

> *There* **shall be allowed** *as a deduction all the ordinary and necessary expenses paid or incurred during the taxable year in carrying on any trade or business* . . . [of the taxpayer].

Any time the word "shall" appears in tax law, it is a Congressional mandate. It means that *all* proper deductions *shall be allowed*. Unfortunately, the IRS takes a different view. Often, it goes out of its way to undo what Congress has legislated.

This is what this book is all about: Telling you what deductions you are entitled to, and forewarning you against IRS efforts to disallow them.

For deduction orientation purposes, you should think of your job expenses as being separated into four classes, namely:

Class I — Occupational (maintaining skills) expenses

Class II — Business (employer necessitated) expenses

Class III — Travel (away overnight) expenses

Class IV — Moving (to a new job) expenses

Once you have oriented your job-expense thinking into these four classes, you are in a better position to appreciate why certain expenditures can be deducted. Many employers these days — beset by regulatory mandates from all levels of government — are "squeezing" employees into paying more and more of the ordinary expenses of operating a business. The result, often, is that employees pay the employers' expenses without taking advantage of the tax deduction potentials.

Thus, our overall objective in this book is to provide you with authoritative information and guidelines that will help strengthen your resolve to use Form 2106, whenever applicable. By doing so, you could be tax money ahead!

CONTENTS

Chapter		Page
1.	**DEDUCTIONS OVERVIEW**	**1-1**
	Tax Home Defined	1- 2
	Commuting Is Personal	1- 3
	Travel Is "Away Overnight"	1- 5
	Separate Tax Homes of Spouses	1- 7
	Memorize These 4 Sections	1- 8
	Must Be "Ordinary and Necessary"	1-10
	The Forms Brigade	1-11
	Temporary Job Assignments	1-13
	Beware of Section 274(d)	1-15
2.	**SCRUTINIZING FORM W-2**	**2-1**
	The 64-Page Mandate	2- 2
	Taxing of Fringe Benefits	2- 3
	Overview of Form W-2	2- 5
	Box 1: Other Compensation	2- 7
	Box 12: Benefits Included	2- 9
	Separate Statement or Multiple W-2s	2-10
	Box 13: See Instructions	2-11
	Correlation of Boxes 1, 12, 13, and 14	2-12
	"Everything" NOT on Your W-2	2-13
3.	**OCCUPATIONAL EXPENSES**	**3-1**
	Designate "Occupation" With Care	3- 2
	Miscellaneous Deductions Role	3- 3
	"Income" Defined by Reg. 1.212-1	3- 4
	Job Hunting Expenses	3- 5
	Certain Educational Expenses	3- 7
	Example Court Rulings	3- 8
	Union Dues & Publications	3-10
	Work Tools & Safety Items	3-11
	Uniforms & Maintenance	3-13
	Seminars and Conventions	3-15

Chapter		Page
4.	**TRADE OR BUSINESS EXPENSES**	**4-1**
	"Trade or Business" Defined	4- 2
	Overview of Section 162	4- 3
	Regulation 1.162-1: For Starters	4- 5
	Tools, Supplies, Et Cetera	4- 6
	Computers and Cellulars	4- 9
	Certain Deductions Limited	4-10
	Other Listed Property Items	4-11
	Gifts & Promotional Items	4-13
	Attendance at Conventions	4-14
	Active Discussion Meals	4-16
	Entertainment: Tough Rules	4-18
	Only 50% M & E Deductible	4-21
	Local Business Destinations	4-22
5.	**TRAVELING EXPENSES**	**5-1**
	Section 162(a) Revisited	5- 2
	Segregated Travel Accounting	5- 3
	The "Primary Purpose" Rule	5- 6
	Business/Personal Allocations	5- 7
	Simple 8-Hour Example	5- 8
	10-Day Allocation Example	5- 9
	Two or More Destinations	5-11
	Foreign Travel Accounting	5-12
	The "Business Necessity" Test	5-14
	En Route "Allocation" Required	5-16
6.	**MOVING EXPENSES**	**6-1**
	At Least 50 Miles	6- 2
	For Commencement of Work	6- 4
	Time at New Location	6- 6
	"Moving Expenses" Defined	6- 8
	Use of Form 3903 or 3903-F	6- 9
	Reimbursement Precautions	6-11
	Meaning of "Code P"	6-13
	What If Excess Reimbursement?	6-14

Chapter	Page
7. **BUSINESS USE OF AUTO**	**7-1**

    Classed as "Listed Property" 7- 2
    Business Use Percentage 7- 3
    Log All Business Trips 7- 4
    Verifying Odometer Readings 7- 6
    Mileage Entries on Form 2106 .... 7- 8
    Most Expenses Qualify 7- 9
    Standard Mileage Rate 7-10
    Limited Cost Recovery 7-11
    Luxury Auto Leasing 7-13
    Leased Auto "Inclusion Tables" 7-14
    Employer-Provided Autos 7-17

8.	**BUSINESS USE OF HOME**	**8-1**

    Self-Motivated, Self-Doers Only 8- 2
    Introduction to Section 280A(c) 8- 3
    Regular and Exclusive Use 8- 5
    Principal Place of Business 8- 6
    Much To-Do About *Soliman* 8- 7
    The One Sensible Opinion 8-10
    Get Statement from Employer 8-11
    Business Use Percentage 8-13
    List Your Operating Expenses 8-16
    Depreciation of Home Structure 8-17

9.	**REIMBURSEMENT & RECORDS**	**9-1**

    Reimbursement Variations 9- 2
    Keep Separate Records 9- 3
    Expense Accounting to Employer 9- 4
    The Regulatory Language 9- 6
    Federal Per Diem Allowance 9- 8
    Prepare for "Full Substantiation" 9- 9
    "Adequate Records" Defined 9-11
    Annotating and Cataloging 9-12
    Separate Reimbursement File 9-13

Chapter	Page

10. MASTERING FORM 2106 10-1

Purpose of Form 2106	10- 2
Start on Page 2: Vehicle Expenses	10- 4
Actual Expense Entry Items	10- 6
Overview of Page 1/Part I	10- 8
General Business Expenses (Line 4)	10-10
The Reimbursement Quandary (Step 2)	10-11
Allocating Your Reimbursements	10-13
What If "Excess" Reimbursement?	10-15
The Line 9, Column B Clincher	10-16
The 50% M & E Law	10-16
Last Item on Form 2106	10-18

11. DEPRECIATION DEDUCTIONS 11-1

Recovery Classes: Employee Property	11- 2
MACRS Methods & Conventions	11- 4
Now for "Listed Property"	11- 6
The Section 179 Election	11- 9
Introduction to Form 4562	11-10
Form 4562: Listed Property Portion	11-11
Form 4562: The Section 179 Portion	11-12
Form 4562: MACRS Portion	11-15
Office-in-Home Depreciation	11-16
Transference to Form 2106	11-17

12. SCHEDULE A (1040) WRAP-UP 12-1

Overall Role of Schedule A	12- 2
Where Form 2106 Is Entered	12- 4
The Lines After Form 2106	12- 6
The 2% AGI Subtraction Law	12- 8
Anticipate/Refine Your AGI	12- 9
The "Standard Deduction" Threshold	12-10
The 3% "Phase Out" Law	12-12
An AMT "Add Back"	12-13
A Cautious Prediction	12-15

1

DEDUCTIONS OVERVIEW

> Code Sections 162, 212, And 217 Direct That Qualified Job Expenses "SHALL BE ALLOWED AS A DEDUCTION" . . . On Annual Forms 1040. Qualified Expenses Are Those Which "Maintain And Improve Skills" In Your Occupation, And Which Are "Ordinary And Necessary" For Carrying On The Trade Or Business Of Your Employer. The Expenses Must Originate At Your Place Of Employment — YOUR TAX HOME — And May Include Travel On Temporary Assignments Away Overnight. When Claiming The Expenses, As Many As 8 Different Tax Forms Can Be Involved. This Requires Extra Effort, But The TAX SAVINGS Can Be Worth It.

In our Introduction, we stressed that the IRS will go out of its way to disallow your job expense deductions. One reason the IRS takes such an adversarial stance is the Internal Revenue Code. The IRS simply has to point its finger at Section 262(a): *Personal, Living, and Family Expenses.* This section reads in part as—

Except as otherwise provided . . ., no deduction shall be allowed for personal, living, and family expenses.

The "otherwise provided" relates to property taxes, mortgage interest, medical expenses, charitable contributions, etc., which have nothing at all to do with job expenses.

To more objectively isolate personal expense matters from job expense matters, a whole body of tax terms has evolved. This

DEDUCTING JOB EXPENSES

definitional body attempts to confine job expenses to those activities that are directly instrumental in producing tangible taxable income. In other words, if, as an employee, you produce income that the IRS can tax, you are entitled to deduct certain expenditures that are "ordinary and necessary" in producing that income. The expenses you deduct must be real and verifiable.

Two specific sections of the tax code confirm your right to the allowability of your job expenses. These two confirmations are, respectively, **Section 162**: *Trade or Business Expenses*, and **Section 212**: *Expenses for Production of Income*. We want to familiarize you with these two sections in this chapter, and also make you aware of the tax distinctions between your tax home and your personal home.

In addition, we want to introduce you briefly to the various tax forms that are necessary when claiming your deductions. Since these deductions can reduce the net tax you pay to the IRS, you should be realistic enough to realize that the IRS will insist that the proper forms be filed. Don't begrudge the forms, nor the work required to complete them. Instead, think of the forms as an opportunity to display your expertise in your chosen work.

"Tax Home" Defined

For tax purposes, we all have two homes. We have a tax home, and we have a personal home. The purpose and function of a tax home are separate and distinct from that of a personal home.

A personal home is where one eats and sleeps on a regular basis, and at which family activities occur. A personal home is for personal living; that is, for spending money which one has earned elsewhere. Its physical size and shape are limited, generally, to a particular building on a particular property site. As one's domicile for personal living, it enjoys certain fundamental rights, such as privacy and so on.

A "tax home," on the other hand, is much broader in concept. It is one's place of business, place of employment, or post of duty. It is the place where one *earns* his living, on a daily and ongoing basis. It is a general area which is not limited to a particular building or property site. As such, it is not protected by fundamental rights

DEDUCTIONS OVERVIEW

such as privacy. The only right that one has at his tax home is the freedom to earn taxable income in whatever manner he can.

One's tax home, therefore, is the point of origin and the point of completion of all job allowable expenses. The frequency of said expenditures is of no concern. The only concern is that they be *business necessitated* for earning one's livelihood at his tax home.

The physical and functional separation of one's tax home from his personal home is a basic and fundamental concept of long standing. So important is this separation concept that we are presenting a pictorial representation of it in Figure 1.1. Also therein, the distinguishing features of the two homes are summarized. Note the opposite directions of the dollar signs: earning money . . . and spending it.

The Figure 1.1 separation is mandated by inference in Section 262 (quoted above in part). Otherwise, nowhere else in the tax code, nor in IRS regulations, is the concept of "tax home" defined. The concept has evolved from many, many Tax Court decisions ruling on the allowableness of job expenses. The clear consensus now is that one's tax home is his **place of employment**; it has nothing whatsoever to do with his lifestyle.

Commuting Is Personal

Everyone knows what "commuting" is. It is the transport of one's self from his personal home to his tax home, and back again. It makes no difference whether one has two tax homes and one personal home, or two personal homes and one tax home. Any transport from any personal home to any tax home, and return to a personal home is commuting. All commuting — no matter what the circumstances are — constitutes a personal expense. No job expense deduction whatsoever is allowed.

Commuting is a personal expense whether one uses a bus, trolley, subway, taxi, limo, boat, airplane, or auto. If there is no public transportation between one's personal home and his tax home whereby one is "forced" to use his own car, it is still not a job expense. If an employer provides commuting transportation on a regular basis, and for some reason the service is unavailable on a

DEDUCTING JOB EXPENSES

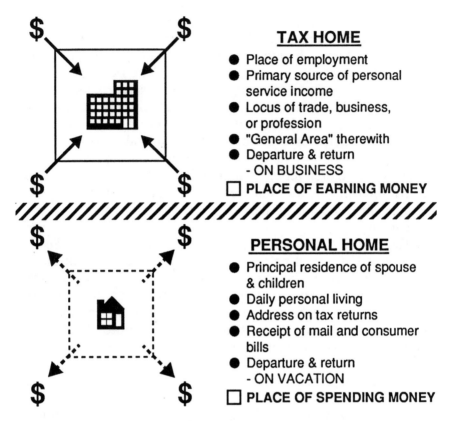

Fig. 1.1 - Fundamental Differences Between Your "Two Homes"

particular day, and one substitutes his own car for that day, it is still commuting (personal).

If one is employed on a regular shift, and returns to his personal home for the evening, and then gets an emergency call to return to work, that, too, is commuting. Distance, and the number of times to and from a tax home, are irrelevant.

Over the years, there have been good-cause efforts to carve an exception to the commuting expense rule. But to no avail. In one case [*Clark*, TC Memo 1978-276], there was no public transportation. The taxpayer was deaf and blind; he could not get a driver's license. His daily use of a taxicab was held to be commuting. In another case [*Brown*, TC Memo 1983-726], the taxpayer, for racial discrimination reasons and harassment, was

DEDUCTIONS OVERVIEW

forced to move to a distant area from his employment. The Tax Court held that there was no provision for any commuting expense deduction based on racial circumstances. In still another case [*Krambo*, TC Memo 1980-425], the taxpayer was a city inspector who carried 75 pounds of tools in the trunk of his car. His contention was that his automobile itself was a tool which he had to have at his tax home, in order to cart his tools to citywide inspection sites. Here, again, the Tax Court held that all expenses from and to his personal home were commuting. He could have left his tools at his tax home.

There are only two (partial) exceptions to the commuting rule. One exception is for those "additional expenses" of commuting for carting bulky equipment and tools which cannot fit into an ordinary passenger car. If one has to use a truck or trailer for carting his equipment and tools, the additional operating cost over that of a regular auto becomes an allowable job expense deduction.

The other exception is for temporary work assignments beyond the general area of one's tax home, where the expense of daily commuting is cheaper than the expense of meals and lodging at the temporary work sites [*Schmidt*, TC Memo 1977-376]. Distance *is* a factor in this exception, to the extent that commuting is sustainable without jeopardizing effectiveness of the worker at the temporary sites. In one precedent-setting case, this distance was limited to 85 miles from the worker's tax home [*Harris*, TC Memo 1980-56]. Otherwise, sleep or rest away from home overnight are required. Rest overnight is a key feature distinguishing travel from commuting.

Traveling between one tax home and a second tax home on the same day is a job expense: not personal. We portray this distinction in Figure 1.2. As you can sense, commuting mileage and commuting expenses must be positively *segregated out* of any mixture of business and personal transportation.

Travel Is "Away Overnight"

In everyday usage, the word "travel" is taken to mean some form of transport from point A to point B. In the tax world of

DEDUCTING JOB EXPENSES

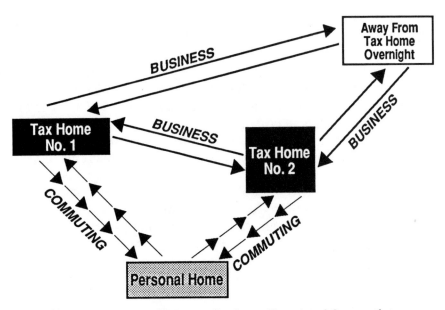

Fig. 1.2 - Distinction Between Business Travel and Commuting

allowable deductions, however, the word is applied exclusively to being away from one's tax home overnight. It is the *overnight* feature that controls: not the away from home. We've already portrayed this feature to you in Figure 1.2.

The tax code section — namely: 162(a)(2) — allowing travel expenses away from home does not use the term "overnight." Nor do the regulations thereunder. The term has evolved from numerous Tax Court decisions over the years. Overnight is determined by the amount of time necessary for "sleep or rest."

A taxpayer is traveling away from home if his duties require him to be away from the general area of his tax home for a period *substantially longer than* an ordinary day's work. During his time off while away, he needs to get sleep or rest to meet the demands of his work. He does not have to be away for a full 24-hour day, or from dusk to dawn. His relief from duty need only be long enough to get necessary sleep or rest [*Johnson*, TC Memo 1982-2].

How long is "long enough" for necessary sleep or rest?

Certainly a full eight hours of sleep or rest in a hotel or motel would qualify. It has also been held that at least five hours of sleep

DEDUCTIONS OVERVIEW

or rest in a 6-hour period of release from duty satisfies the "overnight" tax requirement. Whether the rest period occurs during local nighttime hours is immaterial. It is the duration of rest that counts; not the particular hours.

Release from duty does not require any formal approval. Sleep or rest is the customary practice between two full regular work schedules. Whether the sleep/rest occurs in a 24-hour or 48-hour time span makes no difference. Whatever the time span involved, if there is no adequate sleep/rest period, one is *not* away from his tax home overnight.

The sleep/rest rule eliminates catnaps, short stopovers, stopping at rest areas, stretching out in transportation vehicles, or lying down on benches in airports and train terminals. To qualify as adequate sleep or rest, one must get undressed and into bed.

Let us illustrate. Suppose you took a long airflight to and from a bona fide business destination. You left at 6 a.m. and arrived in time for a good 5-hour business meeting. You returned home at 12 p.m., after "sleeping" on the plane both ways. Do you meet the sleep or rest requirement?

No, you do not. But if the plane had sleeping berth facilities, and you paid extra for a berth, you would meet the test.

The sleep/rest "overnight" rule is important because it determines whether your meals and other expenses (such as laundry, tips, phone calls, supplies, clothing repairs, etc.) associated with travel are deductible.

Separate Tax Homes of Spouses

If an employee is married, his spouse may also be an employee with the same or different employer. When claiming job-related expenses, the two spousal workers are two separate taxpayers. This means that there can be two separate tax homes for business deduction purposes. In other words, each working spouse, as a separate income producer, can claim his or her own job expenses independently of the other spouse. This is so whether they file as married jointly or married separately.

Ordinarily, a husband and wife are treated as one taxpayer when they file a joint income tax return. But, when claiming job expense

DEDUCTING JOB EXPENSES

deductions, this "one taxpayer" concept breaks down. Any qualified expense deduction is a per worker right: not a joint right.

It makes no difference whether the spouses work in the same trade or business or not. Nor does it matter that they have the same occupational qualifications. If both spouses claim job-related expenses or travel for business purposes, each has to keep his/her own separate records and claim his/her own separate expenses. This is so, whether they work for the same employer, or travel together or not.

If a husband accompanies his wife on her business trip, the husband's portion is a personal expense, not business. Conversely, if a wife accompanies her husband on his business trip, the wife's portion is a personal expense, not business. The only exception to this "splitting" of personal and business is when both spouses contribute substantially to the same business purpose of the same business trip.

To illustrate the spousal (per worker) travel separation, consider that the husband is a computer systems engineer, and that the wife is a software sales person. Together they attend a hardware/software convention some 2,000 miles away. They each attend different exhibits and seminars during the working hours of the convention, but they eat their meals and share the lodging together. Except for the lodging (which they split down the middle), all other expenses must be itemized separately for each spouse. This also includes airfare (which is issued as two separate tickets), baggage, tips, publications, etc.

The point to keep in mind about spousal job expenses is that tax recognition derives from each worker's own individual occupation. Those expenses which are allowable are for reasons of occupation only . . . whether married or unmarried.

Memorize These 4 Sections

In our Introduction, we urged that you orient your job expense thinking into four distinct classes. For quick review purposes, these four classes are:

    I   — Occupational (maintaining skills) expenses

DEDUCTIONS OVERVIEW

   II — Business (employer necessitated) expenses
   III — Travel (away overnight) expenses
   IV — Moving (to a new job) expenses

We urged that you think in these four classes because, for each class, there is a separate section of the tax code which specifically authorizes your expense deductions. Corresponding to each class, the applicable tax code section is:

   I — **Sec. 212(1):**   *Expenses for production of income*
   II — **Sec. 162(a):**   *Trade or business expenses*
   III — **Sec. 162(a)(2):**   *Traveling expenses*
   IV — **Sec. 217(a):**   *Moving expenses*

We want you to memorize these four Internal Revenue Code section numbers, their functional class, and their general titles. The IRS will not point out these sections to you, nor will it admit that they even exist. It is up to you, as an employee/taxpayer, to discover them and use them on your own.

In subsequent chapters, we'll quote most of the statutory text — and some of the regulatory text — on each of the above four sections. In the meantime, we want you to take comfort in knowing that certain types of expense deductions are allowable, if you go to the effort of claiming them. For example, the preamble wordings to the above sections say—

   Sec. 162 — *There **shall be allowed as a deduction** all the ordinary and necessary expenses paid or incurred . . .*
   Sec. 212 — *There **shall be allowed as a deduction** all the ordinary and necessary expenses paid or incurred . . .*
   Sec. 217 — *There **shall be allowed as a deduction** moving expenses paid or incurred . . .[Emphasis added.]*

Note the common phrase: *shall be allowed as a deduction.* The IRS tends to duck this phrase, so **you** must insist that the IRS abide

DEDUCTING JOB EXPENSES

by it. The understanding, of course, is that your claimed job expenses are bona fide and verifiable.

Must Be "Ordinary and Necessary"

The mere fact that an item of job expense is paid or incurred in a trade or business (Section 162), or for production of income (Section 212), does not — of itself — entitle one to a tax deduction for it. A basic requirement for deductibility is that the expense be ordinary and necessary for carrying on the business activity. The expense must be *both* "ordinary" *and* necessary: not one or the other.

An expense is "ordinary" if it is customary, common, or usual for the particular type of business in question. That is, an expense is ordinary if it is commonly practiced by others in the same line of work as the claimant. What may be ordinary for one type of business may not be ordinary for an entirely different type of business. It's a "facts and circumstances" issue.

Thus, it is possible for an expense to be ordinary even if it is incurred for the first time by the claimant. The point is that if "others do it," it is ordinary. If one uses ingenuity in incurring an expense which others do not incur, but which furthers his business relative to that of his competitors, it is also ordinary. Particularly so if the competitors start incurring the same novel kind of expense.

For example, if one is charged with fraud in a business transaction, it is customary to hire an attorney to defend oneself. If one is in the business of calling on customers, the expense of phoning them ahead of time and treating them to coffee and doughnuts is customary. So, too, are fees paid by a teacher for attending continuing education seminars and institutes.

An expense is "necessary" when it is essential, indispensable, or unavoidable in one's business. Essentiality also includes expenses which are appropriate and helpful. What constitutes essential travel expenses in a business is largely judgmental. Generally, an expense is essential if it protects the business against losses, litigation, and customer ill will.

For example, suppose a salesman voluntarily pays for repair to a product which he sold, even though the customer was at fault. Such

DEDUCTIONS OVERVIEW

an expense could be construed as necessary in order to keep the customer happy. As another example, a field engineer who rents a car to get him to a remote job site, following a customer complaint, also is necessary. The fact that he could have taken a cheaper form of transportation is irrelevant.

The fact that a job expense proves in retrospect to be unwise, does not prevent it from being ordinary and necessary. Not all business expenditures produce the benefits hoped for. If an unwise expense is reasonable, and not clearly lavish or extravagant, it is deductible.

The Forms Brigade

If you want a tax deduction for some alleged job expense, you should know enough that you will not get it, unless you claim it on the right tax form. You can't expect to get a deduction handed to you on a silver platter just because the tax code says: "shall be allowed." You've got to claim it on the right form!

The more diverse your expenses are, the more diverse are the applicable tax forms, and the more lines and parts on a given form that have to be completed. We've already told you in our Introduction that you must use the "long form," namely, **Form 1040**: *U.S. Individual Income Tax Return*. You cannot use the short forms 1040A or 1040EZ, as there is no line or provision thereon for job expense deductions. Therefore, the very first form that you must be prepared to use is Form 1040.

Except for moving expenses to a new job, there is nothing on pages 1 and 2 of Form 1040 itself that suggests that other job-related expenses are deductible. You either have to know from your own experience or from discussions with your associates that such expenses are claimable on **Schedule A** (Form 1040): *Itemized Deductions*. The second line at the top of page 2 of Form 1040 says—

Itemized deductions from Schedule A

But, even this wording doesn't hint that your job expenses are claimable. You have to examine Schedule A to find out.

1-11

DEDUCTING JOB EXPENSES

When you examine Schedule A, you will find in the lower portion a bold-printed heading which reads—

Job Expenses and Most Other Miscellaneous Deductions

At least you know where most of your job expenses can be deducted. They are in the miscellaneous deductions portion of Schedule A.

On examining the miscellaneous portion more carefully, you will read its very first line:

Unreimbursed employee expenses — job travel, union dues, job education, etc. If required, you MUST attach Form 2106 or 2106-EZ. (See instructions.)

Form 2106 is titled: *Employee Business Expenses*, whereas **Form 2106-EZ** is titled: *Unreimbursed Employee Business Expenses*. Now things are starting to get a little hairy. You have to distinguish between those expenses which are reimbursed by your employer, and those which are not reimbursed. Making this distinction will be one of the most difficult tasks of your recordkeeping chores. We'll explain this difficulty more fully in Chapters 9 and 10.

When you read the instructions to Form 2106, you will find mention of two other forms that relate to the expenses claimed on Form 2106. These two supplemental forms are: **Form 4562 — *Depreciation and Amortization***, and **Form 4797 — *Sales of Business Property***. If you have a car, computer, or office-at-home, for example, that you are using for business purposes, you must depreciate these items over their statutory class lives. Here's where Form 4562 is required. If you sell any of these items while being used for business, Form 4797 is required.

If you move from one job to another, or move to your first job, you are entitled to certain moving expenses in connection therewith. You are given a hint to this on page 1 of Form 1040. The moving expense line is near the bottom of the page in the portion labeled: *Adjustments to Income*. The applicable line there reads—

DEDUCTIONS OVERVIEW

Moving expenses. Attach Form 3903 or 3903-F.

Form 3903 is for claiming domestic moving expenses, whereas **Form 3903-F** is for foreign moving expenses. We'll address these two forms (and the applicable rules) in Chapter 6.

Altogether now, we have mentioned eight different tax forms that you need to resort to when claiming job expense deductions. As you'll see later, you will not need to use each of these forms every year. Nevertheless, we summarize the eight forms for you in Figure 1.3. By so summarizing, we hope you realize that if you want a tax deduction for your job expenses, you have to put in extra effort. Otherwise, forego the forms . . . and PAY HIGHER TAXES. The IRS will love you for this. There is no penalty for paying higher taxes than you need to.

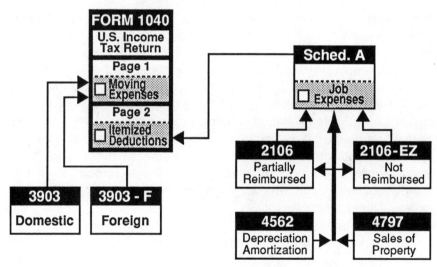

Fig. 1.3 - The "Forms Brigade" for Claiming Job Expenses

Temporary Job Assignments

There is a vast gray area of job expensing which the "brigade" of forms in Figure 1.3 does not adequately address. This gray area has to do with temporary job assignments away from your tax home overnight. The tax issue is: Do you claim these expenses as

DEDUCTING JOB EXPENSES

traveling expenses (Class III) or moving expenses (Class IV), or some combination of both . . . or neither?

Answer: It all depends on the *state of mind* of your employer, each time an away-from-home assignment is made. Is it his intention that the assignment be of temporary duration . . . or something more permanent?

The general tax presumption is that any assignment to a business destination lasting less than one year is "temporary." This presumption is valid only if you do not move your family to that destination to take up residence there. The presumption is valid also only if you indeed return to your predestination tax home. The fact that you may have returned for only a few days, and were reassigned to another business destination, does not detract from the temporariness of your first destination.

There is a special reason why "temporary" assignment is important. It is because there are — or may be — *duplication of expenses* while away from one's tax home **and** while away from one's personal home. For example, while away temporarily you may find it necessary to buy certain tools, rent equipment, purchase materials and supplies, fax and photocopy, buy protective clothing, pay for laundry and cleaning, and make other purchases — besides meals and lodging — which might duplicate those at your tax and personal homes. It is because of this duplication that you are allowed to deduct them when away on business. But, if you move your residence to where your business assignment is, what previously were deductible travel expenses become nondeductible personal and living expenses.

Where business travel is for an extended period of time, say several months or more, there are restrictions on weekend visits to your personal home and family. Weekend visits do not alter your travel status; they just limit the amount of weekend expenditures that are allowable.

If, for business reasons, you remain at your travel destination over a weekend, your meals and lodging are deductible. Whatever amount this is for all-day Saturday and all-day Sunday (or for any holiday period), you are allowed it. This same amount is the maximum deductible when you visit your spouse and children over the same period.

DEDUCTIONS OVERVIEW

For example, suppose the meals and lodging for a Saturday/Sunday weekend at your business destination cost $150 ($60 meals and $90 lodging). The round trip fare to see your family on a weekend is $115. If you don't pay for the business destination meals and lodging, how much weekend travel expenses are you allowed?

Answer: $115; your travel fare only. Your meals and lodging at home are not deductible since you didn't pay for them at your business destination. There are no duplications.

But, suppose you retained the business lodging for the weekend and paid for it (the $90 above). How much travel fare would you be allowed?

Answer: $60. Your allowable total weekend expenses are $150: the same as those at your business destination. Subtracting the $90 lodging from the $150, your weekend travel to see your family is limited to $60.

Beware of Section 274(d)

Count on the IRS to try to disallow most of your job expense claims. It will do so on its premise that you've probably kept inadequate records. Towards this end, it delights in intimidating employees with Section 274(d): *Disallowance of Certain Expenses; Substantiation Required*. So, discipline yourself to prepare good, complete, and convincing records to support your expense claims . . . or else.

The "or else" stance in Section 274(d) reads as follows:

No deduction or credit shall be allowed—
(1) under section 162 or 212 for any traveling expense (including meals and lodging while away from home),
(2) for any item with respect to an activity which is of a type generally considered to constitute entertainment, amusement, or recreation, or with respect to a facility used in connection with such activity,
(3) for any expense for gifts, or
(4) with respect to any listed property [having combined business business and personal use] *. . . unless the taxpayer*

DEDUCTING JOB EXPENSES

substantiates ***by adequate records or by sufficient evidence corroborating the taxpayer's own statement.*** [Emphasis added.]

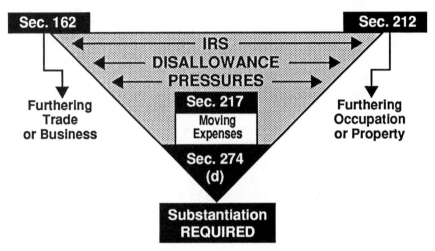

Fig. 1.4 - The Importance of Good Substantiation of Job Expenses

Section 274(d) goes on to detail what constitutes substantiation by adequate records and sufficient evidence. We'll develop these substantiation requirements as we proceed chapter-by-chapter throughout this book. Your first requirement, of course, is to meet the qualifying conditions of Sections 162, 212, and 217. After that, the obvious intent of Section 274(d) is to deny any deduction based on approximation and unsupported testimony.

Job expense substantiation is a critically important concept. So much so that we present our depiction of it in Figure 1.4. As depicted, the practical effect is that of an inverted triangle. If every deduction claim is in perfect balance with applicable rules and regulations, the allowances sanctioned by Sections 162, 212, and 217 will stand. But, if not in perfect balance, your expense claims will fail.

2
SCRUTINIZING FORM W-2

> Unless One Examines Each Form W-2 Carefully, He/She Could Wind Up Paying More Taxes Than Necessary. This Is Because The IRS "Holds A Gun" To The Head Of Every Employer — Via Its CIRCULAR E — To Include Most Fringe And Statutory Benefits As OTHER COMPENSATION In Box 1. Boxes 12, 13, And 14, And Instructions On Copy C, Are Intended To Alert Employees To Form 2106 For Deducting Job-Related Expenses, Where Applicable. The Noncash Items And Cash Reimbursements In Box 1 Too Often Are Overlooked By Employees When Entering The Box 1 Amount On The "Wages, Etc." Income Line On Form 1040.

As an employee, on or before January 31 of each year, your employer is required to provide you with Form W-2. As you already know, this form is titled: *Wage and Tax Statement*. The "wage statement" part summarizes your wages, tips, and other compensation received during the year. The "tax statement" part lists the amount of Federal/State/Local income tax withheld, the amount of Social Security tax withheld, and the amount of Medicare tax withheld. In addition, there is a "miscellaneous statement" part (not in the title) which addresses various statutory benefits (pensions, annuities, deferred compensation, life insurance, etc.) in which you are a participant. All total, there are some **21** boxes of information on your W-2.

DEDUCTING JOB EXPENSES

When preparing Forms W-2 each year, every employer is under intense pressure. The pressure arises from every government agency wanting to control what an employer does with his employees. There are penalties galore! If all 21 boxes on the W-2, where applicable, are not filled out properly, there are penalties. If the withholding amounts are not paid over promptly, there are penalties. Your employer — whether he wants to be or not — is a deputized tax collector for every income taxing agency in the U.S. He gets no compensation whatsoever for this effort.

Furthermore, the IRS is constantly on your employer's back to include on your W-2 all fringe benefits, noncash awards, expense reimbursements, car allowances, educational assistance, and other generally nontaxable amounts. By forcing your employer to do this, the IRS hopes that you will blindly pay tax on these items. To minimize your being deceived by the IRS, we want you to examine your W-2 more inquiringly than you ever have done in the past.

The 64-Page Mandate

Before your employer can prepare Form W-2 for the ending calendar year, he has to procure from the IRS its *Circular E: Employer's Tax Guide*. This is a 64-page publication loaded with directives, special rules, and withholding tables. There are 24 pages of 2-columnar text (comprising approximately 35,000 words), and 40 pages of tables and charts. The text gives tax law reminders, outlines the withholding duties of employers, sets calendar due dates (for tax forms and tax deposits), and defines who are employees.

A main section labeled: *Who Are Employees?* reads in preamble part—

> *Employment status under common law.* — *Anyone who performs services is an employee, if you, as an employer, can control what will be done and how it will be done. This is so even when you give the employee freedom of action. What matters is that you have the legal right to control the method and result of the services.*

SCRUTINIZING FORM W-2

In a subsection to the above: *Treating employees as nonemployees*, your employer is warned that—

You will be liable for income tax and employee social security and medicare taxes if you don't deduct and withhold these taxes because you treat an employee as a nonemployee. See Internal Revenue Code section 3509 for details.

Code Section 3509: ***Determination of Employer's Liability for Certain Employment Taxes*** is an effort by the IRS to force all workers into being classified as employees. This is so that each "deemed employee" can be tax controlled through his/her "deemed employer," regardless of the type of independent services that might be performed. The IRS would like nothing better than to have every worker in the U.S. a "deemed employee" for tax collection purposes. Already, nearly 75% of all federal income tax revenue is withheld by employers as deputized IRS agents.

Why are we telling you this?

Answer: Because the IRS "points a gun" at the head of every employer. As a result, your employer is going to put every penny of compensation, every expense reimbursement, and every fringe benefit that he can on your W-2. This way, he'll withhold from you the maximum tax possible and turn it over to the IRS. Thereafter, it is up to you to sort things out of your W-2, and claim them as job expense deductions wherever you can.

Taxing of Fringe Benefits

Over the years, various fringe benefits given to employees by employers were all treated as freebies. As such, they were tax deductible by the employer and not tax includible (nontaxable) by the employee. Being nontaxable to employees meant that the benefits were **not** reported to the IRS on Forms W-2.

Today, with so much competition among employers to offer fringe benefits, things are different. There are now two distinct classes of fringe benefits: taxable and nontaxable. The taxable fringes *are* reported on your W-2s; the nontaxable fringes are not.

2-3

DEDUCTING JOB EXPENSES

The few nontaxable fringes that are left are those expressly excludable from an employee's gross income by IRC Section 132. Subsection 132(a), *Certain Fringe Benefits: Exclusion from Gross Income*, reads in full as—

*Gross income shall **not** include any fringe benefit which qualifies as—*

    (1)   no-additional-cost service,
    (2)   qualified employee discount,
    (3)   working condition fringe,
    (4)   de minimis fringe,
    (5)   qualified transportation fringe, or
    (6)   qualified moving expense reimbursement.

Any fringe benefit that your employer gives you, which is not included on your W-2, is fully nontaxable. Being "nontaxable" means that such benefits cannot possibly qualify as deductible job expenses. This is so, even if you incurred additional expenses in connection with them.

As to taxable fringe benefits, Circular E (Employer's Tax Guide) specifically says [to your employer]:

Unless the law says otherwise, you [the employer] *must include fringe benefits in an employee's gross income. The benefits are subject to income and employment taxes* [social security and medicare]. *Fringe benefits include cars you provide, flights on aircraft you provide, free or discounted commercial flights, vacations, discounts on property or services, memberships in country clubs or other social clubs, and tickets to entertainment or sporting events. In general, the amount you must include is the amount by which the fair market value of the benefits is more than the sum of what the employee paid for it plus any amount the law excludes. There are other special rules you and your employees may use to value certain fringe benefits.*

Ordinarily, as an employee, you do not see the above IRS language. So, put yourself in the position of your employer for the

SCRUTINIZING FORM W-2

moment. Reading the above about taxable fringes, what would *you* do in cases of doubt? Chances are, you'd do just like your employer would do. You'd report all tax questionable fringe benefits on each employee's Form W-2. Then, you'd leave it up to each employee to decipher the consequences.

This is exactly what most employers do. They have their own tax battles with the IRS. They can't take on your tax battles, too. This is another reason why you must scrutinize your Form W-2 more carefully than ever in the past.

Overview of Form W-2

Most employees take Form W-2 for granted. They've seen these forms so many times over the years that they are oblivious to the IRS tactics taking place. This oblivion is especially costly with respect to job expense reimbursements and job-related fringe benefits, which are mandatory entries for maximum taxation purposes. The oblivion goes on for the simple reason that most employees do not study their Form W-2 very closely . . . if at all. It goes without saying that failure to scrutinize your W-2 will cost you more in taxes than necessary. This is exactly what the IRS has intended. And, it's working!

We know you know what a Form W-2 looks like. Nevertheless, we are going to reproduce it here because we want to call to your attention certain boxes. Accordingly, a slightly edited version of Form W-2 is presented in Figure 2.1. It is "edited" only insofar as the abbreviations of the box headings. As on the official form, all 21 numbered boxes are shown in our Figure 2.1.

Please take a moment to read through all 21 boxes. While doing so, particularly note the boxes that we have emphasized with bold black borders. These boxes are sequentially 1, 12, 13, and 14. We are going to discuss each one of these boxes separately below. We have some things to tell you that you've probably never thought about before.

In the meantime, you are aware, of course, that your employer prepares **six** copies of your Form W-2. These are, respectively:

DEDUCTING JOB EXPENSES

Form W-2	Wage and Tax Statement		Year	
EMPLOYER'S ID	1 Wages, etc. & other compensation		2 Federal income tax withheld	
EMPLOYER'S Name, address, ZIP	3 Soc. Sec. wages		4 Soc. Sec. tax withheld	
	5 Medicare wages		6 Medicare tax withheld	
	7 Soc. Sec. tips		8 Allocated tips	
EMPLOYEE'S ID	9 EIC payments		10 Dependent care	
EMPLOYEE'S Name, address, ZIP	11 Nonqual plans		12 Benefits in Box 1	
	13 See instructions		14 Other	
Copy C - for - EMPLOYEE'S RECORDS	15 Pension plans, etc. □	□□□□□□		
16 State	17 State Wages, etc.	18 State Income Tax	19 Locality	20 Local Wages, etc.	21 Local Income Tax
	Employer's State ID				

Fig. 2.1 - Edited Version of Employee's Form W-2

Copy A — For Social Security Administration
Copy B — For attachment to your Federal return
Copy C — For your own tax records
Copy D — For your employer's payroll records
Copy 1 — For your State Tax Department
Copy 2 — For attachment to your State return

You receive copies B, C, and 2 only. After you file your federal and state returns, you are left with Copy C. It is officially designated:

For EMPLOYEE'S RECORDS (See Notice on back)

It is Copy C that we want you to focus on, especially that notice on the back. Have you ever read that *Notice to Employee*? If not, you should. But, unfortunately, it usually is in small, faded print which is hard to read. This is why we are calling your attention to certain boxes that we emphasized in Figure 2.1.

SCRUTINIZING FORM W-2

Box 1: Other Compensation

Officially, Box 1 on Form W-2 reads—

Wages, tips, other compensation.

It's that "other compensation" part that we want to address. Wages and tips are pretty self-explanatory. The "other compensation" is a catchall for miscellaneous taxable items including job expense reimbursements and job-related fringe benefits.
When you read the "Notice to Employee" about Box 1, the IRS instruction says—

Enter this amount on the wages line of your tax return.

When you look at a Form 1040 (the income tax return on which you claim job expenses on), it reads—

Wages, salaries, tips, etc. Attach Form(s) W-2.

The Form 1040 wages line is the very first taxable income line on your return. So, whatever is in the "other compensation" part of Box 1 is automatically taxable. Now you know why the IRS puts a gun to the head of your employer. He is forced to pack into Box 1 every conceivable form of "other compensation" that he can. Whatever he puts in, he gets a business expense deduction for it.
Your employer's instruction to Box 1 differs markedly from your instruction to the same box. Whereas your instruction consists of just 11 words, your employer's instruction consists of approximately 280 words. Your employer is given eight itemized instructions, of which three are pertinent to our subject. These three pertinent items are:

- *Total noncash payments (including **certain** fringe benefits).*
- ***Certain** employee business expense reimbursements.*
- *All other compensation, including **certain** scholarships and fellowship grants and taxable payments for moving expenses.* [Emphasis added.]

DEDUCTING JOB EXPENSES

Note in all three of these instructional items the use of the word "certain." This is the IRS's tip-off to your employer that there are bona fide areas of uncertainty. Quite often, your employer gives up and "puts in everything." Because everything in Box 1 becomes an automatic business deduction for your employer, it is not taxable to him. However, It is taxable to you, Therefore, it is up to you to decipher for yourself what's in Box 1.

Fortunately, there is a quick way for you to determine the amount of "other compensation" in Box 1. Look at your paycheck stub for the last pay period of the year. Look for the cumulative YTD (year to date) gross wages. Subtract this amount from the figure in Box 1 of your W-2. The difference, if any, is your other-than-wage compensation for the year. Because this is an important precaution you should take, we depict it graphically in Figure 2.2.

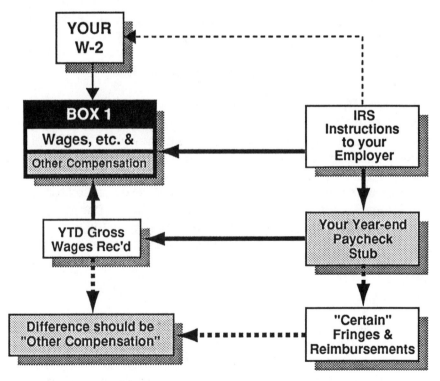

Fig. 2.2 - Verifying the "Other Compensation" Amount in Box 1

SCRUTINIZING FORM W-2

Box 12: Benefits Included

Box 12 on Form W-2 is officially labeled:

Benefits included in Box 1.

Exactly what are these benefits that have been included in Box 1? You have to read that "Notice to Employee" on Copy C of your Form W-2 to find out.

Your Copy C instructions to Box 12 read—

If there is an amount in Box 12, you may be able to deduct expenses that are related to fringe benefits; see the instructions for your tax return.

You go to your Form 1040 instruction booklet for items relating to the "Wages line" on your return. There are about 900 words there. On skimming through, you'll run across a paragraph with the bold letters: ***Employer-provided vehicle.*** The principal portion of this paragraph reads—

*If you used an **employer-provided vehicle** for both personal and business use and 100% of its annual lease value was included as wages on your W-2 form, you may be able to deduct the business use of the vehicle on Schedule A. But you must use **Form 2106**, Employee Business Expenses, to do so.*

This is your first official tip-off that at least some of the Box 1 "other compensation" could be a deductible business expense. But look at how much fine-print reading you have to do to find out about this. If you are too nonchalant and don't read the IRS instructions, you miss this job-expense-deduction authority altogether. Could this be what the IRS is hoping you'll do?

As to Box 12, your employer is IRS instructed to—

Show the total value of the taxable fringe benefits included in Box 1 as other compensation. . . . If you provided a vehicle and included 100% of its annual lease value in the employee's

2-9

DEDUCTING JOB EXPENSES

income, you must separately report this value to the employee so the employee can compute the value of any business use of the vehicle.

In the above instructions to you and to your employer, the term "annual lease value" appears. What do you suppose this means? It means that you and your employer have to look at a special IRS table that *lease values* all vehicles (up to $60,000) at their acquisition market values. Where do you find this special IRS table? Answer: You'll have to ask your employer about this.

Separate Statement or Multiple W-2s

Further, with regard to your employer's preparation of your Form W-2, the IRS instructions to Box 12 say—

You may use a separate statement, Box 14, or multiple Forms W-2, if necessary, to report all Box 12 entries.

The implication here is that your employer must provide you with a "report" of all items, the monetary amount of which is entered in Box 12. The use of Box 12 is an effort to tell you what forms of "other compensation" are included in Box 1. A "report," however, is merely an accounting; it is not an explanation or instruction as to what you are to do.

Some employers use a separate statement in their own computer format to report the items in Box 12. Others use Box 14 (on the Form W-2) which has about three times the space of Box 12.

Box 14 is officially labeled: *Other*. This is a spare box which your employer can use, instead of providing you with a separate statement of his own. The IRS instructions to him read—

You may use this box for any other information you want to give your employee. Please label each item.

What are the IRS instructions to **you** regarding Box 14? Answer: There are none! The "Notice to Employee" on your Copy

SCRUTINIZING FORM W-2

C of Form W-2 skips Box 14 altogether. Check this out for yourself.

Some employers use multiple W-2s to provide you a separate report of the Box 12 items that are included in Box 1 (taxable income). Other than repeating your name and ID and your employer's name and ID, a second, third, or fourth W-2 (for the same taxable year) will show entries **only in** Boxes 12, 13, or 14. All other boxes are left blank — or are supposed to be. Otherwise, if Box 1 were duplicated or triplicated, the IRS's computer would insist that you enter double or triple your wages, etc. on your return. If you are issued multiple W-2s, make sure that Box 1 in the second, third, etc. W-2 is indeed blank. If it isn't, call this error to the attention of your employer immediately.

Box 13: See Instructions

Box 13 on Form W-2 is officially labeled:

See instructions for Box 13.

Your instructions to Box 13 say—

Any amount in Box 13 should be (letter) coded. The following list explains the codes. You may need this information to complete your tax return.

This is another official tip-off that you can claim job-related expenses as a deduction on your return. "But," you ask, "what are the Box 13 items that are job expense related?"

The Box 13 instructions list 18 separate code letters, A through T. Only two of these code letters — "L" and "P" — are pertinent to our subject. In your instructions, these two code letters are listed as:

Code L — *Nontaxable part of employee business expense reimbursements*

Code P — *Excludable moving expense reimbursements*

DEDUCTING JOB EXPENSES

The amounts entered as "L" or "P" are truly nontaxable and excludable. They are NOT in Box 1. They are listed in Box 13 so that the IRS's computer will "see" them, in the event you try to deduct them separately as job expenses.

The IRS instructions to your employer comprise about 1,680 words. He has to puzzle over what they mean. Some of the elements of the Box 13 entries have to be included in Box 1. This can be confusing to both the employer and employee. For example, with respect to Code L (Employee business expense reimbursements), the employer instructions say—

Report the amount treated as substantiated; i.e., the nontaxable portion, in Box 13. In Box 1, include the portion of the reimbursement that is more than the amount treated as substantiated.

Elsewhere, about the only clear-cut instructions to your employer are:

Do NOT enter more than three codes in this box. If more than three items need to be reported in Box 13, use a separate statement, Box 14, or multiple Forms W-2 to report the additional items. . . . Use the codes shown with the dollar amount [e.g., L $5,300].

Correlation of Boxes 1, 12, 13, and 14

At this point, you are probably totally confused about the relative purposes of Boxes 1, 12, 13, and 14 on your W-2. Let's see if we can clarify the situation for you.

For general guidance, always keep this one point in mind. The IRS has compelled your employer to include everything possible as "other compensation" in Box 1. Whatever the amount in Box 1 — right or wrong — MUST be entered on your Form 1040 at the *Wages, etc.* income line. You have no choice about it. Otherwise, the IRS's computer will hound you endlessly.

Your only opportunity to correct or back out any overreportings in Box 1 is the amounts reported in Boxes 12 and 13. If you are

SCRUTINIZING FORM W-2

cavalier and nonchalant about these two boxes, you'll pay tax on amounts that you probably could have deducted as job expenses.

Now, for the functional difference between Boxes 12 and 13. Box 12 deals with *fringe benefits*, whereas Box 13 deals with *statutory benefits*. Fringe benefits are those which are peculiar to your own employer's operations policy. Statutory benefits are elective options in the tax code which are available to all employees and employers.

Anything and everything in Box 12 is automatically included in Box 1. In contrast, most of the amounts in Box 13 are *excluded* from Box 1. They are listed in Box 13 primarily for your information and attention purposes.

Box 14 is simply a "floater" on Form W-2. It gives your employer a little extra space for adding an entry or two for Boxes 12 and 13.

In Figure 2.3, we try to show the correlation of all four boxes (1, 12, 13, and 14) just discussed. By presenting Figure 2.3 in the manner that we have done, we are deliberately trying to direct your attention to Boxes 12 and 13 primarily. These are your "alert boxes." Knowing that some of the displayed amounts are already in Box 1 as taxable income, you should want to study Boxes 12 and 13 carefully. If you can reasonably associate these amounts with job-related expenses, by all means take the extra effort and precaution necessary to back them out of Box 1. You can officially do this via Form 2106: Employee Business Expenses.

"Everything" NOT on Your W-2

We may have given you the impression above that your employer reports *all forms* of "other compensation" in Box 1 of your W-2. True, he is compelled to enter many things. But he is not compelled to enter everything. There are all kinds of expense-related items incurred by employees over which he has considerable discretion. Much depends on his operations policy with regard to business-type reimbursements to his employees.

For example, suppose you submit an expense report to your employer for, say, $3,000. Because of your employer's own rules on what he'll reimburse and what he won't, he reimburses you only

DEDUCTING JOB EXPENSES

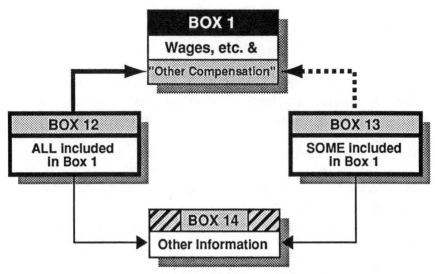

Fig. 2.3 - The Two "Alert Boxes" on Form W-2

$2,500. He does not have to report this amount in Box 1

However, **you** need to keep records on the entire $3,000: The $2,500 reimbursed *and* the $500 not reimbursed. The common mistake is that most employees keep records only on the $500 of unreimbursed expenses. This practice causes major accounting problems when preparing Form 2106: Employee Business Expenses. This form requires that your total expenses be claimed (both reimbursed and unreimbursed), after which you subtract out the reimbursed amounts. The subtraction line reads—

*Enter amounts your employer gave you that were **not** reported to you in Box 1 of Form W-2.*

In the example above, if you claim only the $500 unreimbursed expenses and subtract the $2,500 reimbursed amount, what happens? The IRS's computer will **impute** that you have $2,000 (2,500 – 500) of unreported Box 1 income! You will be taxed and penalized accordingly.

When it comes to job expenses — BOTH reimbursed and unreimbursed — you've got to be on your toes at all times.

3

OCCUPATIONAL EXPENSES

> All "Ordinary And Necessary" Expenses For Performing, Maintaining, Or Improving Skills In Your Established Occupation Are Deductible. This Is The Gist Of Section 212: **EXPENSES FOR PRODUCTION OF INCOME**. Included Are Educational Courses, Job-Hunting Activities, Dues And Publications, Work Tools, Protective Clothing, Safety Equipment, Uniforms, Physical Exams, Seminars, And Other Expenditures Required As A Condition Of Employment. Allowability Is Contingent Upon CONTINUITY In The Same Occupation And The ANNUAL NEED For Sustaining Your Livelihood.

Occupational expenses are those which we categorized as Class I in Chapter 1. They are those expenses which are necessary for maintaining and improving skills in your chosen occupation. As such, they are *skills-related* expenses. They are incurred by a worker in order to be able to hold himself/herself out to an employer as being qualified to do a designated job. These are the types of expenses associated with your occupation, rather than being associated with your employer's particular trade or business.

The IRS classifies skills-related expenses as "nonbusiness." This terminology carries the adverse implication that such expenses are not deductible. To the contrary, they ARE deductible. They are deductible under IRC Section 212: ***Expenses for Production of Income***. The IRS uses the term "nonbusiness" so as to distinguish Section 212 expenses from Section 162: ***Trade or***

DEDUCTING JOB EXPENSES

Business Expenses. Because there is much overlapping between these two sections, job expenditures under either one are deductible.

Skills-related expenses cover a broad spectrum of expenditures quite independent of the nature of the trade or business of one's employer. The spectrum includes professional dues, union dues, books and publications, hand tools, uniforms, seminars, certain educational courses, training and supplies, certain legal fees, and other expenses associated with bargaining for and collecting a worker's income. These kinds of expenditures occur across all levels of occupation, from the highest paid surgeons and airline pilots to engineers, teachers, ministers, police, firefighters, plumbers, electricians, salespersons, librarians, and so on. Every type of income production involves the need for skill-related expenditures to one extent or another.

Designate "Occupation" With Care

If you intend to claim any form of job expenses as a tax deduction, you must use Form 1040. This form accepts Schedule A: Itemized Deductions, with provisions for attaching Form 2106: *Employee Business Expenses*.

If you'll recall Form W-2 in Figure 2.1 for a moment, you will find nothing there that requests or designates your occupation. But, if you will look at the bottom of page 2 of Form 1040, at the signature block, you will see two spaces there. The two spaces are identified as—

Your occupation _____
Spouse's occupation _____

Note that each entry space asks for the designation of "occupation." It does not ask for your title, position, salary grade, or nature of business of your employer. It asks for **your** occupation. If you are married, and filing a joint return together, you are also asked for the occupation of your spouse. The obvious reason for the two occupational spaces is that each spouse may have — separately from the other — qualified skills-related expenses.

OCCUPATIONAL EXPENSES

Whatever the nature of your job expenses, you want to designate your occupation with care. Preferably, choose two words that come closest to identifying your skills. For example, instead of indicating "teacher" or "nurse," use "high-school teacher" or "registered nurse," as appropriate. Other two-word examples are: college professor, patent attorney, second pilot, flight attendant, master plumber, iron worker, outside salesman, interior designer, dance instructor, highway patrolman, and so on.

Don't use fancy-sounding titles or positions. For example, don't use such terms as: vice president, department manager, construction superintendent, etc., even if that is your position in the company. You're not trying to impress the IRS (it's not impressionable anyhow). If you are a department manager, for example, use the functional name of your department, such as customer relations, direct marketing, production engineering, systems analyst — you get the idea. You want to imply that there are special skills in your occupation for which you have incurred legitimate expenses in connection therewith. You also want to imply that you have skills in recordkeeping, and skills in claiming your expense deductions appropriately. You are just not going to be psyched out by the IRS.

Miscellaneous Deductions Role

From the early beginnings of Form 1040, the IRS has taken the position that an employee is not "carrying on" a trade or business for tax deduction purposes. (The requirement for "carrying on" is a Section 162 feature, which we'll get to in Chapter 4.) As a consequence of this IRS position, any skills-related expenditures for one's occupation as an employee had to be treated as *Miscellaneous Deductions* on Schedule A (Form 1040). There is historical legal precedent for the IRS's position.

In the landmark case of *Eugene Higgins* (41-1 USTC ¶ 9233, 312 U.S. 312), the Supreme Court held that the taxpayer was not in a trade or business for tax deduction purposes. Mr. *Higgins* had extensive investments in real estate and securities; he maintained offices in New York and Paris; and he expended monies for cablegrams, telephone, mail, keeping records, getting investment

DEDUCTING JOB EXPENSES

advice, and collecting the income from his investments. He was allowed, however, to deduct most of these expenses as a nonbusiness deduction on Schedule A (1040). This was an indirect form of deduction, rather than a direct deduction as in the case of business expenses by an employer.

Subsequent to the *Higgins* case, **Section 212** emerged. This section, as indicated earlier, is titled: ***Expenses for Production of Income***. It is under this umbrella section that an employee's occupational expenses are allowed. This section reads in full as—

> *In the case of **an individual**, there shall be allowed as a deduction all the ordinary and necessary expenses paid or incurred during the taxable year—*
> *(1) for the production or collection of income;*
> *(2) for the management, conservation, or maintenance of property held for the production of income;* ***or***
> *(3) in connection with the determination, collection, or refund of any tax.* [Emphasis added.]

Note that Section 212 focuses strictly on "an individual." This can be *any* individual: employee, nonemployee, unemployed — anyone who is not acting as a business entity reaching out to the public at large.

"Income" Defined by Reg. 1.212-1

IRS Regulation 1.212-1 is titled: ***Nontrade or Nonbusiness Expenses***. This is another way of saying "miscellaneous expenses." The regulation is comprised of 16 subregulations which have been on the books, essentially unchanged since 1965. A few excerpts from these subregulations will give you the gist of what kind of income is envisioned for Section 212 deduction purposes.

Subregulation (a) says, in part—

> *An expense may be deducted under section 212 only if—*
> *(1) It has been paid or incurred by the taxpayer during the taxable year (i) for the production or collection of income when,*

OCCUPATIONAL EXPENSES

if and when realized, will be required to be included in income for Federal income tax purposes, . . . ; and

(2) It is an ordinary and necessary expense for any of the purposes stated in [Section 212].

Following the above vein, subregulation (b) says—

The term "income" . . . includes not merely income of the [current] *taxable year but also income which the taxpayer has realized in a prior taxable year or may realize in subsequent taxable years.*

And, further, subregulation (d) says—

*Such expenses must be reasonable in amount and must bear a **reasonable and proximate relation** to the production or collection of taxable income.* [Emphasis added.]

On reading these subregulations, it is self-evident that any amount that goes into Box 1 of Form W-2: *Wages, tips, other compensation* (recall Chapter 2) is the type of income against which job-related expenses may be deducted. The deduction applies not only to current-year income, but to prior- and prospective-year incomes as well. This certainly covers all expenses attributable to maintaining and improving skills in your current occupation.

Job Hunting Expenses

One occupational issue that frequently comes up has to do with job hunting expenses by employees, new employees, former employees, and unemployeds. The "income" concept (in the subregulations above) implies that, before any expense deduction can apply, there has to be some *reasonable and proximate* taxable income therewith. What happens in those situations where there is no income that can be associated with the expenses incurred — such as looking for a job?

DEDUCTING JOB EXPENSES

The answer has to do with the concept of *continuing* one's present (or former) occupation. If you are already qualified for a specific occupation, and have been once employed in that occupation, the fact that you may be unemployed, or seeking other employment, does not change your occupational status. If, for example, you are an airline pilot, software engineer, or science teacher who is unemployed at the moment, all expenses incurred in looking for a job — IN THE SAME OCCUPATION — are deductible. This is because your expenses are associated with the income of your **occupation** (past, present, prospective), and not with a particular employer.

But if you are a brand new hire (just out of school or college) or are seeking to change your occupation (an airline pilot wanting to become a securities broker), your job hunting expenses are NOT deductible. Why? Simply because you have no prior, present, or immediately prospective income in your new occupation.

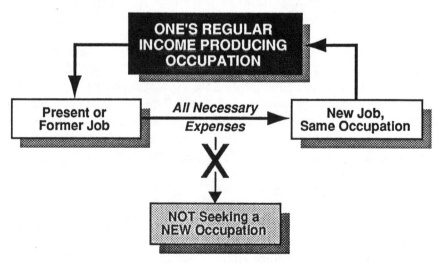

Fig. 3.1 - The "Continuation Concept" for Job-Hunting Expenses

The IRS and the Courts (Tax Courts, particularly) have consistently held to these positions since as early as 1954. The central concept, which we depict in Figure 3.1, is that you must be in — or have been in — a designated occupation, and that you are seeking continuation in that same occupation. If you qualify in this

OCCUPATIONAL EXPENSES

regard, all job hunting expenses therewith — employment agency fees, resumés, supplies, phone, mail, transportation, etc. — are allowable. They are allowable, even if you've had several unsuccessful job interviews.

On this point, the Form 1040 instruction booklet, Schedule A: *Unreimbursed Employee Expenses*, says—

Examples of expenses to include are:

- *Fees to employment agencies and other costs to look for a new job in your present occupation, even if you do not get a new job.*

Certain Educational Expenses

In the same vein as "continuing in your present occupation," certain educational expenses are allowed. Two specific conditions, however, must be met. Deductible education expenses are those which—

1. Maintain or improve skills (in your present occupation), or
2. Meet the express requirements of your employer (in your present occupation).

The IRS regulation on point is Regulation 1.162-5: *Expenses for education*. The pertinent wording is—

Expenditures made by an individual for education (including research undertaken as part of his educational program) which are not expenditures of a type described in paragraph (b)(2) or (3) ... are deductible ... (even though the education may lead to a degree) if the education—

(1) Maintains or improves skills required by his employment ..., or

(2) Meets the express requirements of the individual's employer, or the requirements of applicable law or regulations, imposed as a condition to the retention by the

3-7

DEDUCTING JOB EXPENSES

individual of an established employment relationship, status, or rate of compensation.

Essentially, deductible educational expenses are limited to refresher courses, updating and upgrading courses, new developments, advanced training, and specialized programs offered by academic and vocational institutions. The expenses allowable include tuition, books, supplies, tools, fees, transportation, etc.

Nondeductible educational expenses (as defined in paragraphs (b)(2) and (b)(3) of Reg. 1.162-5) are those for attaining the minimum educational requirements of a job, or those for qualifying for a new occupation differing from one's present job. This all reverts back to the underlying concept depicted in Figure 3.1. One must be in an EXISTING employable occupation, deriving income therefrom, before his expenses are deductible.

Example Court Rulings

Whether one continues in his same occupation or changes to a new one through self-improvement requires analysis on a case-by-case basis. Certainly, if a uniformed police officer studies to become an attorney in criminal law, he has changed his occupation. But what about a classroom teacher who becomes the school principal? Is this a change of occupation? No; it is a change of duty in the same occupation: the teaching profession. To help explain the governing rationale involved, we present below a few randomly selected court cases — out of literally thousands of disputive issues that occur yearly.

> A pilot of a C-130 aircraft who took flight training courses which led to his obtaining an FAA flight engineer's certificate for the Boeing 727 and an airline transport pilot certificate for the C-130 was entitled to deduct his expenses for the course which led to the pilot certificate but not the expenses for the flight engineer courses. The obtaining of an airline transport pilot certificate was not a minimum requirement for his employment, nor did it qualify him for a new occupation (as the flight engineer's certificate would have).
> — *N.L. Mason*, 44 TCM 365, Dec. 39,159(M), TC Memo 1982-376.

OCCUPATIONAL EXPENSES

An unlicensed accountant was allowed a deduction of 80% of his educational expenses for tuition, books, and related travel. Four of the five courses he took maintained and improved his skills, but the accounting course was a prerequisite to sitting for the CPA examination and therefore was not deductible. This fifth course would have prepared the taxpayer for a new position in the accounting profession.
— *H.S. Cooper*, 38 TCM 955, Dec. 36,146(M), TC Memo 1979-241

The tuition etc. expenses incurred by a paramedic firefighter to obtain a bachelor of science degree in organizational behavior were not deductible since the courses qualified the taxpayer for many new occupations. Also, expenses for algebra and physics courses were not deductible since the courses (1) did not maintain or improve the skills of a firefighter, and (2) did not meet the express requirements of the firefighter's employer.
— *D. Barboza*, 62 TCM 417, Dec. 47,539(M), TC Memo 1991-379.

Expenses incurred by a hospital orderly and ward clerk in pursuing a master's degree in hospital administration were not deductible since the degree qualified him for a new occupation as hospital administrative assistant. The scope of duties performed by an orderly and ward clerk and a hospital administrative assistant is significantly different.
— *J.D. Hogue*, 37 TCM 126, Dec. 34,919(M), TC Memo 1978-17

An attorney was not entitled to deduct a real estate course and a fee for taking the real estate broker's examination as educational expenses because such expenditures qualified the attorney for a new occupation of being a real estate broker.
— *D.A. Goldstein*, 52 TCM 1481, Dec. 43,659(M), TC Memo 1987-47

The key rationale to all the above is spotting the "present occupation" of each individual. The minimum length of time for being in a present occupation is not specified anywhere. However, a number of rulings have indicated that, if it is less than a year, it is not regarded as a livelihood-type occupation. It is treated as a temporary activity until a more permanent occupation is acquired.

DEDUCTING JOB EXPENSES

Union Dues & Publications

Once you are established in a livelihood-type occupation, other ordinary and necessary expenses are allowed. Among these are expenditures for union dues, professional dues, trade magazines, technical publications, research journals, new development periodicals, and the like. Your Form 1040 instruction booklet merely lists these allowables as—

- *Union dues*
- *Dues to professional organizations*
- *Subscriptions to professional journals*

You need more narrative information than this.

The term "dues" — for tax deduction purposes — applies strictly to labor unions and professional organizations. These entities generally limit their membership to persons who are presently qualified in the occupation which each entity represents. Being of the same or similar occupation, all dues-paying members benefit from the common representation and from the mutual exchange of information between themselves. The common goal is to advance the occupation. Because of this commonalty of occupational interests, union dues and professional dues are "skills related" — for income purposes. As such, the dues are deductible.

This commonalty of occupational interests does not apply to club dues. A "club" is an association of individuals of different occupations who have common interests in athletic, recreational, social, fraternal, pricing, or philanthropic activities. The tax code is very emphatic that club dues are not deductible. On this point, Section 274(a)(3): **Denial of Deduction for Club Dues**, reads—

> *Notwithstanding the preceding provisions of this subsection, no deduction shall be allowed . . . for amounts paid or incurred for membership in any club organized for business, pleasure, recreation, or other social purpose.*

This seems pretty clear to us. The phrase "Notwithstanding . . ." refers to pre-1994 rulings where focused deductions were allowed

OCCUPATIONAL EXPENSES

for "active pursuit of business" cases. But no more. From 1994 on, club dues are out.

Actually, union and professional dues are allowed only to the extent that they are assessed on a monthly or annual basis. In turn, the dues must be used for the day-to-day operations of the membership group. This requirement eliminates initiation fees, special assessments (for pension, welfare, or building improvements), and other charges which represent long-term rights in the organization. It is the *annual use* feature of dues money that makes them deductible.

A similar "annual use" concept applies to expenditures for magazines, periodicals, journals, and other publications that specialize in the occupational activities of the purchaser. To be deductible, these items must have an informational life of a year or less. They are printed materials which are intended to be read, with perhaps a few pages removed, and then thrown away. Clearly, this excludes reference-type books and texts which have a shelf-life more than one year. Longer-than-a-year books and texts must be designated as one's "professional library," then depreciated (rather than expensed).

To summarize the gist of the features that we have just discussed, we present Figure 3.2. In some occupations, such as in medical, legal, accounting, educational, marketing, and other fields, expenditures for dues and publications can be substantial.

Work Tools & Safety Items

Within the context of meeting express "worker readiness" requirements of one's employer or of an applicable regulatory agency, expenditures for work tools, protective clothing, safety articles, and sundry items are deductible. This deductibility is because, as part of one's minimum qualification for a job assignment, he is expected to have minimal tools and items to perform that job. You wouldn't expect a carpenter, for example, to appear at a construction site without, at least, a hammer, staple gun, and skill saw. And so it is with other occupations, regardless of income level.

DEDUCTING JOB EXPENSES

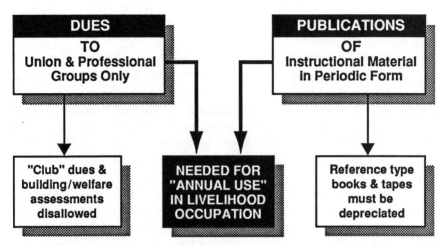

Fig. 3.2 - Why Certain Dues and Publications are Deductible

On this subject, your Form 1040 instruction booklet lists the deductibles as:

- *Safety equipment, small tools, and supplies you needed for your job.*
- *Protective clothing required in your work, such as hard hat, safety shoes, and glasses.*
- *Physical examinations your employer said you must have.*

Note use of the term "small tools." This raises the question: How small is "small"; how big is "small"? There are two answers: (1) the tax answer, and (2) the practical answer.

From a tax point of view, a work tool is small if it costs no more than $100 and its useful life is no more than one or two years. Otherwise, it has to be depreciated. The minimum depreciation classlife designated by IRC Section 168(e)(1) is three years (for items lasting more than two years).

From a practical point of view, a small tool is one which is readily transportable by hand, either carried on or nearby the person using it. It is an item subject to rapid wear, breaking, or being stolen. Its cost must be definitely less than $1,000 for each item. The term "small" also includes replacement tools of the same kind, spare parts, accessory attachments, repairs, and maintenance.

OCCUPATIONAL EXPENSES

Protective clothing and safety equipment (again if "small") are two variants of the expectation that a qualified worker have with him his necessary hand tools. Protective clothing is that which (generally) **goes over** a worker's ordinary street clothing, such as rain gear, wind breakers, rubber boots, smocks, face masks, rubber gloves, and the like. Its purpose is to protect against inclement weather or germs in the workplace.

In contrast, safety equipment comprises those special items that are necessary when working under hazardous conditions. Such conditions occur when handling toxic materials, chemicals, nuclear wastes, molten metals, and the like. Safety items are also needed when working at great heights, great depths, in tunnels and caves, and in other hostile environments. Items included are safety belts, gloves, shoes, hard hats, goggles, bulletproof vests, X-ray shields, wet suits, parachutes, fire extinguishers, gas masks, etc. Most of these items are "small" when paid for by the employed worker himself. If the employer pays for any of these items, they, of course, are deductible by the employer: not by the employee.

In those occupations where public safety is an issue, periodic physical examinations of a worker (when paid for by the worker) are deductible expenses. The transportation industry is the one most subject to regulatory requirements concerning the physical fitness and mental alertness of workers. The most commonly affected occupations are airline pilots, railroad engineers, bus drivers, marine vehicle operators, and highway patrolmen.

Uniforms & Maintenance

The term "uniforms" is not even mentioned in the tax code. Yet, it has a distinctly popular meaning of its own. A "uniform" is an item of attire that, when worn in the workplace, distinctively signifies that the wearer is "on duty" on behalf of his employer. That is, it is distinctive from ordinary street clothing. Often, one or more insignias attach to a uniform to indicate the rank and position of the wearer, and the employer for whom he works.

It is generally recognized that the cost of purchasing uniforms and accessories, and their cleaning and maintenance, are deductible

DEDUCTING JOB EXPENSES

job expenses. The deductibility, however, is contingent upon the following tests, namely:

(1) The uniforms must be of a type specifically required as a condition of employment.

(2) They must not be adaptable to general or continued usage to the extent that they take the place of ordinary clothing.

(3) They must not be worn regularly as a substitute for street clothing, but only as necessary to get to and from work.

On this subject, your Form 1040 instruction booklet, although acknowledging that certain expenses are deductible, simply says—

- *Uniforms your employer said you must have, and which you may not usually wear away from work.*

This is a rather broad statement. It leads to bona fide misunderstandings as to what constitutes deductible uniform expenses. What about designer clothing and entertainment apparel required by one's employer?

In a defining case [*B.D. Pevsner,* CA-5, 80-2 USTC ¶ 9732, 628 F2d 467], a boutique manager was required to purchase and wear designer fashions while at work. Away from work, the manager did not wear the designer clothes because they did not conform to her everyday lifestyle. The Court denied the extra clothing expenses as a job deduction. It reasoned that because the clothing was utilitarian and worn by a significant, although affluent, segment of society, such clothing was appropriate for general or personal wear. The fact that the manager chose not to wear it apart from work was based on her personal choice and lifestyle.

The same utilitarian reasoning applies to coveralls and other protective clothing worn in place of regular clothing. If an item is purchased to protect one's regular clothing, rather than to protect one's self against bodily injury, the expense is usually not deductible. This is usually the case for such ordinary items as

OCCUPATIONAL EXPENSES

coveralls, khakis, blue jeans, grubbies, slacks, and other off-the-shelf types of work clothes. Clearly, these items are not uniforms.

In view of the above, it is tax important to understand the rationale for distinguishing between uniforms, protective clothing, safety apparel, and customary street wear. We try to summarize this rationale for you in Figure 3.3.

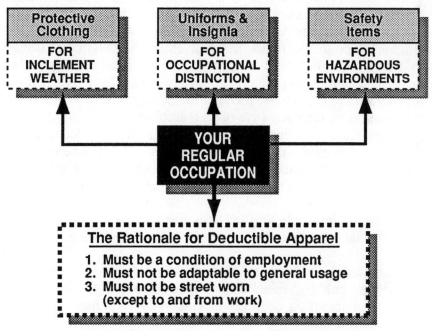

Fig. 3.3 - Distinguishing Features for Deductibility of Wearing Apparel

Seminars and Conventions

A "seminar" is a one-afternoon, one-evening, or one-day meeting of like-occupation individuals to hear a speaker on a designated subject related to their occupation. Opportunity is afforded for the audience to ask questions of the speaker, and to engage in a brain-storming of ideas among members of the audience. If this is what you think of as a seminar, and you attend one or more such events during the year, your expenses therewith are deductible. Treat them as "professional development" expenses.

DEDUCTING JOB EXPENSES

As occupationally-oriented seminars, such meetings are a form of education for maintaining/improving your skills as an employee.

A "convention," on the other hand, is a two- or three-day affair, at which display booths, exhibits, and demonstrations appear. It is an industry-wide event to which a broad range of different occupational skills are invited. Usually, there is a banquet-type luncheon or dinner at which some renowned speaker addresses the convention goers. A convention is characterized by a greater social element, camaraderie, and opportunity to meet new people, than at a seminar. The theme focus of a convention is intended more for your employer's benefit than for your interest as an employee. As such, the expenses you incur may or may not be deductible. Much depends on the motivation for your attending, and on whether you are a designated representative of your employer.

As you recall, earlier in this chapter we stated that occupational expenses are deductible under Section 212 (Expenses for Production of Income). Yet, Section 274(h)(7), which addresses attendance at seminars and conventions, states flat out that—

No deduction shall be allowed under section 212 for expenses allocable to a convention, seminar, or similar meeting.

Compare this flat-out prohibition with what your Form 1040 instruction booklet (Schedule A: Miscellaneous Deductions) says. Under the subsection headed: **Examples of Expenses You May Not Deduct**, it says—

- *Expenses of attending a seminar, convention, or similar meeting **unless it is related to your employment**.* [Emphasis added.]

The above message is: When you incur expenses for seminars and conventions, you must show a direct relationship to your employment. Your "employment" is different from your occupation. The term employment involves the interests of your employer and his consent to your attendance on his behalf.

4

TRADE OR BUSINESS EXPENSES

> Employees Are Allowed All Necessary Expenses For "Carrying On" An Employer's Trade Or Business. These Include The Cost Of Tools, Supplies, Uniforms, Safety Equipment, And "Et Cetera" Items PLUS Registration Fees, Publications, Postage, Public Stenographer, Computer Rentals, Transportation, And More "Et Ceteras." Deductions For Purchases Of Computers, Cellulars, Electronics, And Office Furniture And Furnishings Are Subject To LISTED PROPERTY Rules Requiring The Establishment Of A BUSINESS USE PERCENTAGE For Each Item Over 3, 5, Or 7 Years. Stringent Rules Apply To Business Meals And Entertainment, With The Result That ONLY 50% Of All M & E Expenditures Are Allowed.

Trade or business expenses are those which we categorized as Class II in Chapter 1. They are those expenses which you as an employee incur on behalf of your employer. You are incurring them to pursue and promote the profit-seeking interests of your employer's business. As such, they are *business-related* expenses.

Whereas occupational expenses (Chapter 3) focus on your skills as an employee, business expenses focus on the profit or loss aspects of your employer's enterprise. If your employer does not have at least some modicum of success in his enterprise, you may not have a job to which to apply your skills. Consequently, it is important that you promote your employer's interests to the fullest extent of your job status and description.

DEDUCTING JOB EXPENSES

To be tax deductible by you, the business expenses must have been paid or incurred by you. This means that you have to itemize the expenses and keep adequate records on them. When you do, most employers will reimburse you for those expenses, to one degree or another. After which, it is the NET amount — expenses less reimbursements — that is deductible by you.

The authority for allowability of your net business expenses is Section 162: *Trade or Business Expenses*. The essence of this tax code section is rather straightforward: all necessary expenses *in carrying on* any trade or business shall be allowed. It is this "carrying on" phrase that permits employees to be included.

Yet, as straightforward as its essence is, Section 162 is THE MOST LITIGIOUS and quarrelsome section of the entire Internal Revenue Code. Of the nearly 1,800 basic tax laws, Section 162 comprises in excess of 750 pages of regulatory text and rulings briefs. The nearest other section with so much attention is Section 61 (Gross Income Defined). But it has "only" 385 pages of regulatory and rulings text. Our point is that, when you have a bureaucracy such as the IRS administering a straightforward law, interpretations can become unduly complex. A lot of restrictive conditions are applied, which do not always make common sense. Unless you are made aware of some of these restrictive conditions, you may wind up spending money for your employer and get no tax deduction for it.

"Trade or Business" Defined

The term "trade or business" is a statutory phrase that goes back to the early beginnings of income tax law. It even precedes the 1913 constitutionalization of income taxes. It goes back to the colonial origin of trade marks and trade names. These were symbols and logos used for identifying merchandise and products traded in interstate and international commerce. As a result of this long history, today the phrase "trade or business" is embedded in tax concrete.

In general terms, a trade or business is an activity — any activity — carried on for income or profit. To qualify as such, the activity must be pursued full time, in good faith, and with regularity. Goods

TRADE OR BUSINESS EXPENSES

and services of some kind must be offered to the public, with the expectation of producing income to the business entity. Whether there is net profit or net loss is not the point. Bona fide business activity can produce a loss and still be allowed its expenses in connection with that loss. The presumption is that, if a business loses money several years in a row, the owners will either cease that business, reorganize, or change to another business.

The operational form of business is not determinative as to whether a trade or business exists. The form may be a proprietorship, partnership, corporation, or any derivative therefrom. What matters is that there is an owner (or owners) of the business, that it engages one or more employees, and that it seeks contact with its customers and suppliers on a regular and ongoing basis. In most cases, the existence of an employer-employee relationship is itself indicative of a trade or business.

As a point to note, trade or business expenses are deducted differently by employers and employees. For an employer, the business expenses that he incurs — including most reimbursements to his employees — are an "above the line" deduction. This simply means that he gets to claim his expenses *directly* against his gross income, before arriving at his taxable income.

In contrast, an employee gets to deduct his business expenses "below the line." The so-called "line" is one's **total income** on his Form 1040. A below-the-line deduction is *indirect* and less advantageous than an above-the line deduction. As an employee, several filtering conditions are imposed to reduce the net effectiveness of your business expense deductions.

The above-below line concept to which we refer is depicted in Figure 4.1. Since this book is intended for employ**ees** rather than for employers, we'll sidestep any and all discussion of your employer's business expense deductions. In many respects, though, they are not too different from your deductions.

Overview of Section 162

Tax Code Section 162 is titled: ***Trade or Business Expenses***. We know that we have mentioned this section title several times up to this point. We have done so intentionally. We want you to

DEDUCTING JOB EXPENSES

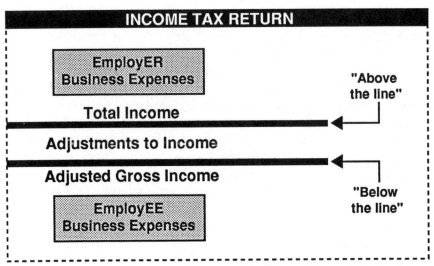

Fig. 4.1 - "Above/Below Line" Concept for Business Expense Deductions

memorize the section number and title words. It is THE most important job expense deduction authority that you have. It's leadoff sentence is: *There shall be allowed as a deduction . . . etc.*

Section 162 consists of about 5,000 statutory words, arranged into 15 separate subsections: (a) through (o). Most of the subsections are directed at employers — mostly large employers. Many of the subsections have no direct bearing on the types of expenditures incurred by ordinary employees. For example, the following subsections speak for themselves as to whom they are directed:

    Subsec. (c)   — Illegal bribes, kickbacks, and other payments.
    Subsec. (e)   — Denial for certain lobbying expenditures.
    Subsec. (g)   — Treble damage payments under antitrust laws.
    Subsec. (h)   — State legislators' travel away from home.
    Subsec. (j)   — Certain foreign advertising expenses.
    Subsec. (m) — Certain excessive employee remuneration.
    Subsec. (n)   — Special rule for certain group health plans.

Subsection 162(m) is interesting. Its paragraph (1) says, in essence, that—

TRADE OR BUSINESS EXPENSES

> *... no deduction shall be allowed ... with respect to any employee ... [whose] remuneration for the taxable year ... exceeds $1,000,000* [1 million].

We're quite sure that no employee in this over-$1,000,000-compensation category will be reading this book. Consequently, we can skip over many/most of the subsections in Section 162.

With the above in mind, let's quote to you the portions of subsection 162(a) that are pertinent to ordinary employees, namely:

> *There shall be allowed as a deduction* [in computing taxable income] *all the **ordinary and necessary** expenses paid or incurred during the taxable year **in carrying on** any trade or business, including—*
> *(1) **a reasonable allowance** for salaries or other compensation for personal services actually rendered; ...*
> [Emphasis added.]

In Chapter 1, we explained the meaning of "ordinary and necessary" as being those expenses which are essential to the success of a business. The "carrying on" phrase means that a business must be in existence and continuing. The "reasonable allowances" for salaries, etc., means that employees should be paid no more than is commensurate with their contributing skills, and, as such, they, too, become part of the "carrying on" of the business.

So far, so good. The above quoted statutory wording seems to make sense, don't you think?

But are you aware that it takes approximately 240 pages of regulatory text to interpret subsection 162(a)(1) in terms of everyday business practices? The IRS doesn't allow a business expense deduction just because you, as an employee, claim it to be such.

Regulation 1.162-1: For Starters

The IRS has prepared some 29 separate primary regulations interpreting Section 162. (Actually, there are 26, as three are "held in reserve.") Regulation 1.162-1 is the dominant one, with respect to Section 162(a)(1). This one regulation alone, and its supporting

DEDUCTING JOB EXPENSES

rulings briefs, takes up about 240 pages! For starters, let's quote selected portions of Regulation 1.162-1(a): ***Business expenses.***

This 620-word regulation reads in part—

Among the items included in business expenses are management expenses, commissions, labor, supplies, incidental repairs, operating expenses of automobiles, traveling expenses, advertising and other selling expenses, insurance against fire [etc.], *and rental for the use of business property. No such item shall be included . . . to the extent that it is used in computing the cost of inventory, or used in determining the gain or loss basis of plant, equipment or other property* [of the business]. . . . *The full amount of the allowable deduction for ordinary and necessary expenses in carrying on a business is deductible, even though such expenses exceed the gross income derived during the taxable year from such business.*

Is this a broad enough definition of allowable business expenses for you? The references to "cost of inventory" and "gain or loss basis" are capitalization items which are distinct from the regular operating expenses of a business. Except for the acquisition of depreciable items (autos, computers, faxes, cellulars, etc.) which an employee may purchase and use for the benefit of his employer, the inventory and plant of a business are generally outside the realm of employee-incurred expenses.

In Figure 4.2 we present a complete listing of all regulations promulgated under Section 162. A quick glance-reading at the titles should give you a good idea of the scope of this important trade-or-business-expense section. Obviously, from this point on, we have to limit our discussion to those items which are most likely to be within the purview of employee-incurred expenditures.

Tools, Supplies, Et Cetera

There's quite a bit of overlapping between skills-necessitated expenses and business-necessitated expenses. This is particularly true of tools, supplies, uniforms, and other sundry items. In other words, just about every item described in Chapter 3 (except job-

TRADE OR BUSINESS EXPENSES

IRC Sec.162: Trade or Business Expenses
THE REGULATIONS THEREUNDER

Reg. No.	Title	Subregs.	Word Count
1.162-1	Business Expenses	(a) - (b)	620
1.162-2	Traveling Expenses	(a) - (f)	780
1.162-3	Cost of Materials	-	170
1.162-4	Incidental Repairs	-	140
1.162-5	Expenses for Education	(a) - (e)	3,830
1.162-6	Professional Expenses	-	110
1.162-7	Compensation for Personal Services	(a) - (b)	640
1.162-8	Treatment of Excess Compensation	-	140
1.162-9	Bonuses to Employees	-	140
1.162-10	Certain Employee Benefits	(a) - (c)	110
1.162-11	Rents and Royalties	(a) - (b)	840
1.162-12	Expenses of Farmers	(a) - (b)	890
1.162-13	Depositors' Guaranty Fund	-	200
1.162-14	Advertising and Promostion	-	250
1.162-15	Contributions as Business Expenses	(a) - (d)	530
1.162-16	Subdividing Real Property	-	20
1.162-17	Substantiation of Employees' Expenses	(a) - (e)	2,210
1.162-18	Illegal Bribes and Kickbacks	(a) - (c)	1,950
1.162-19	Capital Contributions to FNMA	(a) - (b)	1,620
1.162-20	Lobbying Expenses	(a) - (d)	3,640
1.162-21	Fines and Penalties	(a) - (c)	1,260
1.162-22	Treble Damages Under Antitrust Laws	(a) - (f)	1,480
1.162-23	"Held in Reserve"	-	-
1.162-24	"Held in Reserve"	-	-
1.162-25	Noncash Fringe Benefits	(a) - (c)	810
1.162-26	"Held in Reserve"	-	-
1.162-27	Remuneration in Excess of $1,000,000	(a) - (i)	9,000
1.162-28	Allocation of Lobbying Costs	(a) - (g)	3,360
1.162-29	Influencing Legislation	(a) - (f)	4,700
	Total Regulatory Words ▶		39,440

Fig. 4.2 - Listing of the 29 Regulations Under Section 162

hunting expenses) can also be trade or business necessitated. When it is so, the expenditure amounts are generally greater. This is because an employer's interests are more diverse and more persistent than an employee's own skills-maintaining interests.

DEDUCTING JOB EXPENSES

Thus, small tools, materials, supplies, professional dues, trade publications, software programs, audio tapes, video tapes, computer discs, postage, stationery, entry fees (to product exhibits: not entertainment), public phone, public stenographer, fax charges, and other miscellaneous expenditures, whether employer-mandated or not, are tax allowable — if business needed. Included in this overall category are uniforms, protective clothing, safety equipment — the works. There is no one rule or regulation that expressly lists all of these items under one category, such as "tools and supplies," "uniforms," "safety equipment," etc. You get the approbative idea from regulatory bits and pieces.

To give you the regulatory flavor of "et cetera"-type expenditures, we present the following excerpts:

Reg. 1.162-1: Business expenses
— Among the items included in business expenses are . . . labor, supplies, incidental repairs . . . advertising and other selling expenses.

Reg. 1.162-3: Cost of materials
— Taxpayers . . . should include in expenses the charges for materials and supplies . . . actually consumed and used in operations during the taxable year.

Reg. 1.162-4: Repairs
— The cost of incidental repairs . . . [to property] . . . which keep it in an ordinarily efficient operating condition, may be deducted as an expense.

Reg. 1.162-5: Expenses for education
— Expenditures made by an individual for education . . . are deductible . . . if the education . . . meets the express requirements of the individual's employer, or the requirements of applicable law or regulation.

There is one precaution to be heeded when claiming overlapping "et cetera" deductions for skills and business. The precaution is: there can be no double deduction. That is, you cannot claim a

TRADE OR BUSINESS EXPENSES

deduction for a specific item under Section 162 (trade or business) while simultaneously claiming it under Section 212 (production of income). When you are dealing with a lot of "et cetera"-type items, it is easy to inadvertently duplicate your listing of those expenses. This is especially likely when assigning the expenses to different cost categories, such as: under $100, $100 to under $1,000, and $1,000 and over. Just use caution.

Computers and Cellulars

There is a distinct class of expenditures which we call "office-type items." This class applies to such items as portable computers (lap tops), desk-top computers, modems, cellular phones, answering machines, fax machines, small copy machines, audio recorders/players, video recorders, film projectors, slide projectors, cameras, portable typewriters, desk calculators, and other electrical/electronic items for recording, storing, retrieving, and playing back business information. For characterization simplicity, we refer to this category of items as *computers and cellulars*.

Generally, the cost of each computer/cellular item ranges upward from $100 to a few thousand dollars or so. In order to enhance their work performance, many employees pay for these items themselves. They then seek reimbursement from, or cost-sharing with, their employer. Regardless of the employer's response, each item acquired is primarily for business reasons. It is clearly helpful to the employer.

Traditionally, the above items have been characterized as "office equipment." This was to distinguish them from heavy-duty machinery and shop equipment for manufacturing processes. But, today, there is such a plethora of electronic devices for business uses at other than the traditional office that new terminology is required. Most of the listed items are small in size, light in weight, and capable of being hand-carried from place to place.

Because of the portable nature of these office-type items, they are vulnerable to personal use and family access. This is where the IRS antennae focus in. The IRS wants to impose its *listed property rules* to disallow as much as possible for any personal use. This, then, becomes another expensing area where precaution is required.

DEDUCTING JOB EXPENSES

Certain Deductions Limited

The computer/cellular items mentioned above are tax classed as "listed property." This means that the amount of deduction allowable is limited by the rules of Section 280F. This section is titled: *Limitation Where Certain Property Used for Personal Purposes*. This is a 2,800-word complex tax law which is poorly organized and not thought through very intelligently. Nevertheless, it is on the books; you need to be aware of its existence.

Subsection 280F(d)(4)(A) defines listed property as including—

(i)   *any computer or peripheral equipment,*
(ii) *any cellular telephone (or other similar telecommunications equipment),*
(iii) *any property of a type generally used for purposes of entertainment, recreation, or amusement, and*
(iv) *any other property of a type specified by the* [IRS].

The common thread throughout all listed property is a mixture — or potential mixture — of business and personal use. For this reason, no deduction is allowed unless a claimant can show convincingly what portion of the use is for business purposes and what portion is for personal purposes. Alleging that it is 100% business use will not do. One must establish the *business use percentage* by adequate records or other sufficient evidence. This usually means keeping some kind of logbook of the total hours the item is used. Of the total hours used, the amount of business use must be documented by showing the time "on/off" and the nature of the business usage.

Once the business use percentage is established for a given year, for a given item, each listed item must be separated into one of two categories. The first category is **more than 50%** business use; the second is **50% or less** business use. The more-than-50% category gets more favorable depreciation-type deduction allowances than the 50%-or-less category.

All computer/cellular items (listed property) which cost more than $100, with a useful life of more than one year, must be depreciated. The depreciable life is 3, 5, or 7 years as designated by

TRADE OR BUSINESS EXPENSES

Section 168(e)(3) of the IR Code. The methods of depreciation are 200% DB (declining balance), 150% DB, or 100% S/L (straight line), depending on "cost recovery" rules. The statutory amount of depreciation is then modified by the business use percentage to arrive at an allowable deductible amount. The various computations have to be entered on Form 4562, Part V: *Depreciation, Listed Property*.

To summarize the factors involved in establishing the allowable deductible amounts for listed property, we present Figure 4.3. We'll tell you much more about Form 4562: *Depreciation, Etc.* in Chapter 11. This form is an important adjunct to your job expense claims for any property item with a useful life in a trade or business more than one year.

Form 4562	Part V	Listed Property - Automobiles, Certain Other Vehicles,, Certain Telephones, Certain Computers, and Property Used for Entertainment, Recreation, or Amusement
(a)		Type of property _____
(b)		Date placed in service _____
(c)		BUSINESS USE PERCENTAGE _____
(d)		Cost or other basis _____
(e)		Basis for depreciation [(d) x (c)] _____
(f)		Cost recovery period _____
(g)		Depreciation method & convention _____
(h)		Depreciation deduction ▶▶▶ _____
		● Do you have evidence to support the "business use" claimed? ☐ Yes ☐ No
		● If "Yes", is the evidence written? ☐ Yes ☐ No

Fig. 4.3 - Information for Establishing a Deduction for Listed Property

Other Listed Property Items

In the statutory definition of listed property above, we omitted (intentionally, then) other types of property items. The important omissions were: (a) passenger automobiles, (b) other transportation

4-11

DEDUCTING JOB EXPENSES

vehicles (air, water, highway), (c) office-at-home (telecommuting), (d) furniture and fixtures (office, lab, shop), and (e) other noncomputer/noncellular items capable of having mixed personal and business use. Typical examples of those "other items" are personally-owned autos, airplanes, boats, ergonomic chairs, ergonomic work stations, video recording equipment, etc.

Section 280F is intentionally anti-employee. Its primary purpose is to discourage claiming job-related expense deductions based on whim and the cavalier attitude of employees. This purpose is evident from the part of the title we omitted above. The omitted part is: *Limitation on Depreciation for Luxury Automobiles*. A "luxury automobile" is one costing more than $12,000! The idea is that if you want a deduction for listed property items, you have to stand your ground and seek the written cooperation of your employer.

On this point, subsection 280F(d)(3)(A): *Deductions of Employee*, reads in full—

> *Any employee use of listed property shall not be treated as use in a trade or business for purposes of determining the amount of any depreciation deduction allowable to the employee (or the amount of any deduction allowable to the employee for rentals or other payments under a lease of listed property)* **unless such use is for the convenience of the employer and required as a condition of employment**. [Emphasis added.]

Please reread the emphasized clause: "convenience of/condition of." It means only one thing. With respect to listed (mixed-use) property, you get no deduction unless you can get a written *convenience/condition* statement from your employer. This means, on company letterhead, a statement describing your job assignment and describing the equipment and location necessary for performing your job. Many employers are reluctant to provide such a statement. This means that you'll probably have to write the statement yourself, then do a little office politicking to get it signed by someone in authority higher than yourself.

Incidentally, an "employee" is a 5-percent owner of your employer's business or a person related to a 5-percent owner. A 5-

TRADE OR BUSINESS EXPENSES

percent or more owner of a business and his relatives are *deemed employees*, whether officially designated as such or not. The presumption is that these persons are using — or could use — company vehicles and other listed property "free." As such, the fair market value of this use must be entered in Box 1 of Form W-2. Then, if any 5% owner or his relatives wants a business deduction for the employer-provided items, said persons have to follow the same listed property depreciation rules that you have to follow [Sec. 280F(d)(6)(C)].

Gifts & Promotional Items

There is one employee expenditure area that bypasses the listed property depreciation rules entirely. This has to do with small gifts and promotional/advertising items dispensed while carrying on business for your employer. Almost all employers expect certain employees to make small gratuitous gifts to good customers and clients, and promotional pitch come-ons to prospective customers and clients. Within certain dollar limits, the cost of these items is tax deductible. That is, provided there is some appropriate relationship between the gift and the economic benefit to the expense claimant.

Traditional examples of deductible gifts are magazine subscriptions, flowers, candy, packaged food, bottles of booze, camera film, artifacts, doodads, Christmas cards, Christmas presents, and the like. So long as these items are given to your customers, clients, suppliers, or prospects, you are not likely to be hassled by the IRS. But if the gifts are to co-workers, elevator operators, parking lot attendants, maitre d's, and others who are not influential to your income stream, they will be disallowed. The allowable gifts can be made in the vicinity of your tax home, or while in a travel status. It makes no difference.

The gifting dollar limit is $25 per person per year. This is an aggregate of all gifts to the same person. There is no limit to the number of persons you can gift to, provided they are within the expanse of your business clientele.

Gifting separately to a husband and wife, or to a customer and members of his family, counts as one person. For example, if you

DEDUCTING JOB EXPENSES

gave a $20 bottle of vintage wine to one of your customers and simultaneously give his wife a $15 bouquet of flowers, you would have made a single $35 gift. Of this amount, only $25 is tax recognized.

The $25 limit is set in concrete in Section 274(b)(1): *Gifts, Limitation*. This section reads in part as—

(1) No deduction shall be allowed under section 162 or section 212 for any expense for gifts made directly or indirectly to any individual to the extent that such expense, when added to prior expenses of the taxpayer for gifts made to such individual during the same taxable year, exceeds $25.
(2) For purposes of paragraph (1), a husband and wife shall be treated as one taxpayer.

The exceptions to this $25 limit are specialty advertising items (pens, pencils, desk sets, souvenirs) and advertising devices (signs, display racks, promotional material) used on or off the business premises of the recipients. Also excepted from the $25 limit are incidental wrapping, shipping, and delivery costs (including tipping the delivery person).

Except for this advertising/delivery exception, you are urged to characterize your recordkeeping of these expenditures as *small* gifts. By using the word "small" you are signaling the IRS that you are well aware of the $25 limit. It's not a bad idea to accompany your small gift records with a list of names of the persons to whom you have given. Include a short statement of what was given.

Attendance at Conventions

In Chapter 3, we pointed out that there was a tax distinction between a seminar and a convention. A "seminar" is generally one or more meetings of like-occupation persons who are seeking — or are required — to enhance their occupational credentials. The benefits, if any, to an employer's business are intangible and indirect.

Attendance at conventions, on the other hand, have a more direct business-related purpose. Employers' products and service are

TRADE OR BUSINESS EXPENSES

displayed, exhibited, demonstrated, and advertised. Samples and business cards are given out. There are tables, trays, or shelves of "Please-take-one" promotional literature. Each exhibitor/employer is trying to pitch his name and logo to all convention attendees. As a consequence, an employee who attends a convention does so as a representative of his employer. As such, his out-of-pocket expenses are considered to be: *directly related to the active conduct of a trade or business*. And, as such, his expenditures are tax deductible.

Out-of-pocket-type expenses necessary for attending a business convention include:

- Admission fees and exhibit fees
- Portering samples and literature
- Incidental materials and supplies
- On-site secretarial/computer services
- Display site snacks and beverages
- Public telephone, fax, and postage
- Laundry, cleaning, and maintenance
- Bulletin board and paging costs
- Purchases of programs, samples, & booklets
- Items lost or stolen on site

The key to the deductibility of convention expenses is found in IRS Regulation 1.274-2(d)(3)(i)(b): ***Meetings at Conventions, Etc.*** The essence of this subregulation is—

> *Any meeting officially scheduled in connection with a program at a convention or similar general assembly, or at a bona fide trade or business meeting **sponsored and conducted by** business or professional organizations, shall be considered to constitute **a substantial and bona fide business** [activity]. . . . The expenses necessary to the attendance . . . [are] ordinary and necessary within the meaning of section 162 or 212 . . . [in] that such program [is] **the principal activity** of the convention, general assembly, or trade or business meeting.* [Emphasis added.]

DEDUCTING JOB EXPENSES

Aside from the out-of-pocket-type expenses above, attendance at conventions can involve travel (away from tax home overnight), meals, and entertainment. Travel and lodging expenses have to be separated from meals and entertainment expenses. Separation is required because different allowability rules apply.

Attendance at local conventions (not away from home) comprises the easiest expense to be allowed. This is because of the local vicinity of the activity. Travel is not involved (local transportation is not classed as "travel"), and ordinary meals are not deductible. Entertainment, if any, is usually the province of key employees and owners of the business, and seldom done by "ordinary employees." Nevertheless, if the business purpose of a convention is **substantial and bona fide**, all of the necessary expenses for attending it are allowable.

Active Discussion Meals

A common expenditure incurred by ordinary employees is the classical "business lunch." This is a mid-day or end-of-day meal (food and beverage) which follows or precedes an *active business discussion* in the general vicinity of the employee's place of business. In tax terminology, these are called "active discussion meals." There is no pretense of entertainment or recreation involved. The expense claimant invites a consultant, customer, client, supplier, vendor, or prospect to meet in a public restaurant where a bona fide business discussion can take place. The employee pays for the meal, pays for the tip, and pays for any parking required.

The deductibility of these active discussion meals is sanctioned by Tax Code Section 274(k): ***Business Meals***. Paragraph (1) thereof reads—

> *No deduction shall be allowed under this chapter for the expense of any food or beverages **unless**—*
> *(A) such expense is not lavish or extravagant under the circumstances, and*

TRADE OR BUSINESS EXPENSES

*(B) the taxpayer (or an employee of the taxpayer) is **present** at the furnishing of such food or beverages.* [Emphasis added.]

What the "no deduction" clause means is that an expense claimant cannot simply pay for someone else's meal, without himself or his representative being present This effectively rules out all "silent" business meals.

The presence of the claimant is to tax-assure that some form of *substantial business discussion* takes place. It is immaterial whether such discussion takes place immediately before, during, or immediately after the meal. In some reasonable manner, the discussion and meal must be closely related in time. We depict this close relationship in Figure 4.4.

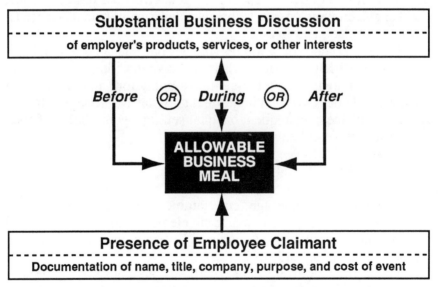

Fig. 4.4 - The "Close Relationship" for Allowable Business Meal(s)

What constitutes a "substantial business discussion"?

Each trade, business, or income-producing activity is different, of course. So the facts and circumstances of each case have to be established on their own. It is clear, though, that the claimant himself/herself has to actively engage in a scheduled meeting,

DEDUCTING JOB EXPENSES

negotiation, discussion, or other specific business transaction. The duration of the engagement must be significant — not incidental — in relation to the subject at hand. Thus, if you spend a concentrated 15 minutes in an arm's-length endeavor, and you reach some reputable understanding or agreement, you've had a substantial business discussion. It is irrelevant whether the related meal itself lasts an hour or two.

What documentation do you need?

First of all, you need to record the business purpose of the meal. This is a nutshell description, such as closing a sale, negotiating a lease, setting a delivery date, complaint against service, and so on.

Next, you need to identify the business person or persons involved (other than yourself). This includes their function and relationship to the business matter discussed. Again, only a brief description is required, such as sales rep, customer relations staff, field engineer, maintenance technician, department manager, foreign business contact, and so on.

There is no tax limitation on whether one eats a large meal or a small meal. Whatever one needs for his own nutrition is acceptable. There is that always-present qualitative limitation: not extravagant or lavish. Unless you habitually eat at 5-star restaurants, dine on gourmet cuisines, or frequent banquet settings, your choice of food and beverage is not likely to be questioned.

Entertainment: Tough Rules

Like food and beverage, entertainment is a customary part of doing business. It is the humanizing element that softens the hard bargaining of profitable negotiations. Entertainment constitutes the "customer relations" side of business.

The term "entertainment" includes any activity generally considered to be entertainment, amusement, or recreation and the use of any facility in connection therewith. It includes entertaining guests at night clubs, cocktail lounges, country clubs, theaters, sports events, and on hunting, fishing, vacation, and similar activities. Entertainment may — and most often does — include food and beverages (particularly alcoholic) at the place of entertainment.

TRADE OR BUSINESS EXPENSES

The IRS views any kind of entertainment as an anathema. They denounce it, condemn it, and disapprove of it with bureaucratic fervor. Your function in life — according to the IRS — is to generate maximum possible tax revenue. Entertainment expenses are a distraction from this IRS-imposed role.

Hence, right up front, we want to forewarn you. When you claim any form of entertainment expenditures — perfectly legitimate though they may be — you do so with your back up against the wall. The IRS gets its power kick from Section 274(a): ***Disallowance of Certain Entertainment, Amusement, or Recreation Expenses***.

The "in general" portion of Section 274(a)(1) reads principally as—

No deduction otherwise allowable . . . shall be allowed for any item—
*(A) With respect to an activity which is of a type generally considered to constitute entertainment, amusement, or recreation, **unless** the taxpayer establishes that the item was **directly related to**, or, in the case of an item directly preceding or following a substantial and bona fide business discussion . . . that such item was **associated with**, the active conduct of the taxpayer's trade or business, or*
(B) With respect to a facility used in connection with an activity referred to in subparagraph (A).
In the case of an item described in subparagraph (A), the deduction shall in no event exceed the portion of such item which meets the requirements of subparagraph (A). [Emphasis added.]

In short and to the point: Entertainment expenses are arbitrarily disallowed UNLESS—

(a) they are *directly related* to the active conduct of your trade, business, or income-producing activity, OR
(b) they are *associated with* a substantial and bona fide business discussion which either precedes or follows the entertainment event.

DEDUCTING JOB EXPENSES

Furthermore, even if you meet these two criteria, your allowable expenses are only those which can be specifically allocated to (a) or to (b). Those expenses which are remotely related or indirectly associated are deemed excess expenses, which are disallowed.

Entertaining at Home

There is no prohibition against an expense claimant entertaining at his personal home, or at other tangible facilities which he may own. His allocable expenses are deductible to the extent that he meets "all of the above" entertainment preconditions. The mere presence of existing or potential customers or clients is not enough. The event must be occasioned by some specific business purpose, which is made known to the guests in advance.

A good example of entertainment at home which was allowed is the Tax court case of *J.R. Howard* (TC Memo 1981-250). The expense claimant was an executive of a communications business: newspapers, radio, and TV. He frequently entertained persons who were prominent in their professions: authors, publishers, artists, actors, stage managers, editors, producers, and the like. Prior to each of his dinner-party events, he initiated a group presentation of his new ideas (with slides, charts, and samples) and sought attendee feedback in the form of comments, suggestions, and criticisms. The meeting room and dining place in his home were free of substantial distractions. The claimant was allowed all expenses in preparing for each event: the cost of his discussion aids, the cost of food, drinks, and catering service, and the expense of cleaning up after the guests had departed. For each event, the claimant kept a list of the names of the persons attending and their professional expertise.

In another Tax Court case (*Progressive Engineering, Inc.*, TC Memo 1975-82), the company owner bought a yacht and tax characterized it as "a floating engineering and sales office." The operator of the yacht was a duly licensed mariner who kept an official log of the daily activities. It turned out that the business-purpose entertainment events were rare. The few events that did occur were not related to nor associated with any substantial business discussion. The use of the yacht for entertainment purposes was to primarily benefit the wife who was the principal shareholder in the closely-held family corporation. All claimed entertainment and operational expenses were summarily disallowed.

For ordinary employees — those below executive level — the need and opportunity for incurring entertainment expenditures is probably minimal to nil. This is because the realm of business entertainment is usually reserved for division heads, vice presidents, and CEOs of a business. Even so, there may be times when you are assigned by your employer to accompany a business associate on a sporting or recreational event. If you receive such an assignment, be sure to keep contemporaneous records (times, dates, places, activities, amounts) of every penny that you spend. Do this, whether you are reimbursed fully by your employer or not.

Only 50% M & E Deductible

The letters "M & E" stand for "meals *and* entertainment. The IRS lumps the two activities together — eating meals and being entertained — as being one and the same. In the functional sense, they are closely related, though not always so. It is not uncommon to participate in an active discussion business lunch without any entertainment whatsoever. The reverse is not so common. Most business entertainment events are accompanied by food and beverage to at least some extent. No matter: meals and entertainment are in the same tax class.

Even with perfect substantiation and justifying records, 100% of M & E expenditures is never allowed. The maximum allowable is 50%. This is set forth very clearly in Section 274(n): ***Only 50 Percent of Meal and Entertainment Expenses Allowed as Deduction.*** Paragraph (1) thereof reads—

The amount allowable as a deduction . . . for—

(A) any expense for food or beverages, and
(B) any item with respect to an activity which is of a type generally considered to constitute entertainment, amusement, or recreation . . .,

DEDUCTING JOB EXPENSES

shall not exceed 50 percent of the amount of such expense or item which would (but for this paragraph) be allowable as a deduction.

There are some modest exceptions to this 50% maximum M & E rule. The few exceptions apply to nonrestaurant settings such as meals provided on an employer's premises, and those included in one-price tickets (such as airline tickets) offered to the general public.

The 50% rule on M & E suggests the following, as a tax planning tip. If you are going to invite business guests to lunch, limit the invitation to a *one-on-one* meeting. That is, take out one invitee at a time. This way, you pay for both meals — yours and his/hers — and get an expense deduction for 50% of the combined cost of both meals (including tips) You can rationalize the 50% disallowance as adjusting for the fact that you have to eat anyhow, whether accompanied by a business person or not.

If you invite two or more persons to a business lunch or other meal, you are paying out of pocket more than just for your own meal. You are paying the disallowed amount for your business guests, too. A better way is to have one (or more) of your employee associates go with you, and each of you pick up the tab for yourself and one guest. If there were three business guests, for example, you should invite two of your working associates to go with you to engage in the business discussion.

Local Business Destinations

The cost of your going to and from a local business destination is 100% allowable as a job expense deduction. No 50% rule applies as in the cases of meals and entertainment. Here, the term "cost" includes *all* costs — out of pocket and equivalent to out of pocket — associated with the transportation process. These costs include taxi fares (and tips), public transportation tickets, parking, tolls, gas, oil, repairs . . . everything except traffic tickets and parking fines. Fines and penalties for violating local law are never deductible.

A "business destination" is a place at which a bona fide business purpose occurs, separate and apart from your tax home (your

TRADE OR BUSINESS EXPENSES

employer's place of business). It is "local" if the destination is in the general (commuting range) vicinity of your tax home. That is, the distance does not involve the necessity for staying away overnight. The "local" is the noncommuting phase of your daily transportation to and from your regular place of work.

Back in Chapter 1, we made a point of telling you that commuting from your personal home to your tax home, and back to your personal home, is a pure personal expense. You get no tax deduction for it whatsoever. No matter how you try to rationalize it, commuting is just not tax recognized as an "ordinary and necessary" business expense. The obvious reason for this is that you can choose your personal home to be wherever you want it to be. Your employer has no control over this.

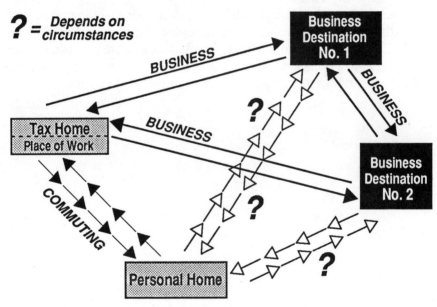

Fig. 4.5 - Local Noncommuting to One or More Business Destinations

But, once you report to your place of work, and leave that place to go to a business destination, you enter the world of non-commute/business transportation. As we depict in Figure 4.5, you may visit any number of business destinations during your work

DEDUCTING JOB EXPENSES

day. As long as a bona fide business purpose is served, all transportation expenses therewith are allowable.

There can be situations where the distinction between commute and noncommute is not all black or white. Suppose, for example, that your normal workday starts at 8:00 a.m. at your employer's place of business. One day, your employer directs that you be at a business destination also at 8:00 a.m. Does this mean that you have to get up extra early and report to your tax home before noncommute departing to your assigned business destination?

Answer: No. Some common sense has to be used — the IRS notwithstanding. If you went from your personal home direct to a business destination and commenced work at about the same time as at your regular workplace, that would be treated as noncommuting business.

Similarly, if you left your business destination at the end of your workday, at about the same time that you would have left your tax home, that, too, would be treated as business transportation. You don't have to go back to your tax home to retrace your regular route of commuting. Again, some common sense has to be used.

5

TRAVELING EXPENSES

> A "Claimant Traveler" Is One Who Is Away Overnight In The ACTIVE PURSUIT Of His Trade Or Business. When So, All Travel Fares, Meals & Lodging, And Directly "Incident-To" Expenses Are Deductible. The Deductibility Of Domestic Travel Is Based On Its PRIMARY PURPOSE Whereas Foreign Travel Is Based On Its BUSINESS NECESSITY. At A Domestic Destination, Each Normal 8-Hour Working Day Must Be Accounted For "Hour By Hour." At A Foreign Destination, A Bona Fide "Business Event" — Regardless Of Its Duration Time — Counts As A Full Business Day. All "On Call" Time At Domestic Or Foreign Destinations Counts As Business Time.

Traveling expenses are those which we characterized as Class III in Chapter 1. They are those expenditures which are necessary when away from your tax home — overnight — in the active pursuit of your employer's trade or business. It is the "overnight" feature that determines whether one is in a business travel status: not just "being away."

As explained in Chapter 1, an employee is traveling on business if his duties require that he be away from his tax home for a period substantially longer than an ordinary day's work. His relief from duty must be long enough to allow him to get necessary sleep and rest, in order to continue his duties the following day. The number of overnight hours is not particularly controlling, though a minimum of at least five hours is considered essential. This amount of time or

DEDUCTING JOB EXPENSES

longer generally requires the use of facilities at commercially established hotels and motels. It is for this reason that the most convincing evidence of travel status is a *lodging receipt*. It alone identifies the destination, date(s), and who the traveler is.

Once the overnight requirement is met, all expenses associated with preparing for the trip, getting to the destination, staying there, and returning from it are deductible. This includes local transportation, air fares, meals and lodging, climatic accessories, laundry and cleaning, phone and faxes, entertainment, gifts, and other "directly attributable" business expenditures.

Section 162(a) Revisited

The tax deduction thrust for all business travel expenditures emanates from Section 162(a): **Trade or Business Expenses**. Actually, it is paragraph (2) of Section 162(a) that expressly addresses traveling expenses. However, presenting paragraph (2) by itself is awkward and misleading. For a full understanding of its role, its preamble and postlude paragraphs must also be presented. Otherwise, you miss the statutory rationale for the allowability of traveling expenses.

The particular statutory wording that we want you to be aware of is as follows:

There shall be allowed as a deduction all the ordinary and necessary expenses paid or incurred during the taxable year in carrying on any trade or business, including—

(2) traveling expenses (including amounts expended for meals and lodging other than amounts which are lavish or extravagant under the circumstances) **while away from home in the pursuit of a trade or business;** *and . . .*

For purposes of paragraph (2), the taxpayer shall not be treated as **being temporarily away from home** *during any period of employment if such period exceeds 1 year.* [Emphasis added.]

TRAVELING EXPENSES

The emphasized phrases are the ones that we want you to memorize. They are the ones that the IRS will try to interpret against you. They also are the phrases that the Courts (Tax Court, District Court, Claims Court) will focus on should there be a protracted dispute between you and the IRS. The IRS tends to act belligerently against all travel claimants. It does so on its presumption that all alleged business travel is a disguise for personal vacation and fun.

Other than being way from home overnight, the key justification for allowability of traveling expenses is . . . IN THE PURSUIT OF . . . a trade or business. The word "pursuit" means actively devoting time and energy to furthering your employer's business interests. Other than time to and from your assigned business destination, you must account, each day, for the *pursuit aspects* of your at-destination time.

The phrase . . . BEING TEMPORARILY AWAY . . . has some subtleties and implications which may escape you. Why is this phrase so tax important?

Answer: Because you are allowed "meals and lodging" (the statutory phrase) and the related personal living expenses while away. Meals and lodging are the kind of personal expenses that all employees incur, whether business traveling or not. By defining what "temporarily away" means, Congress has enacted a cut-off time limit (one year) after which meals and lodging are disallowed. The expectation is that, when an employee leaves his tax home on a business trip, he will return within a reasonable period of time to resume his normal duties. Otherwise, after one year, an employee is considered to have moved to a new tax home.

Segregated Travel Accounting

Whereas many employees incur occupational and trade or business expenses in the vicinity of their tax homes, far fewer employees incur traveling expenses. This fewer number is because business travel is the province of senior technical and customer relations staff, sales and marketing personnel, department and division heads, and executives and owners. These persons are the ones who generate and perpetuate the ongoing interests of the trade

DEDUCTING JOB EXPENSES

or business which they represent. While many of these persons are experienced travelers, they are not all attuned to the importance of segregated travel accounting for tax deduction purposes.

The key elements of segregated travel accounting can be found in IRS Regulation 1.162-2(a). This regulation is titled: ***Traveling Expenses***, and addresses deductible travel as follows:

> *Traveling expenses include travel fares, meals and lodging, and expenses **incident to travel** such as expenses for sample rooms, telephone and telegraph, public stenographers, etc. Only such traveling expenses as are **reasonable and necessary** in the conduct of the taxpayer's business and **directly attributable to it** may be deducted. If the trip is undertaken for **other than business purposes**, the travel fares and expenses incident to travel are personal expenses and the meals and lodging are living expenses. If the trip is solely on business, the reasonable and necessary traveling expenses, including travel fares, meals and lodging, and expenses incident to travel, are business expenses.* [Emphasis added.]

If you dissect this regulatory paragraph into its common sense terms, you'll find that the expenses incurred for each travel event ("the trip") are to be broken down into three categories, namely:

1. In-transit costs,
2. Meals and lodging, and
3. Incident-to costs

And, where personal and business activities are mixed, the costs have to be further broken down into—

- Business expenses, and
- Personal expenses.

Of course, if a trip is "solely on business" (the regulatory wording), no segregation for personal expenses is required.

What we are leading up to is the importance of **segregating** your travel expenses as you go along. This can be done more

TRAVELING EXPENSES

readily in the travel mode. The details are fresh in your mind then; they are part of your day-to-day activities. All you need to know is the specific segregation categories to use. For mental memory purposes, we depict these categories for you in Figure 5.1.

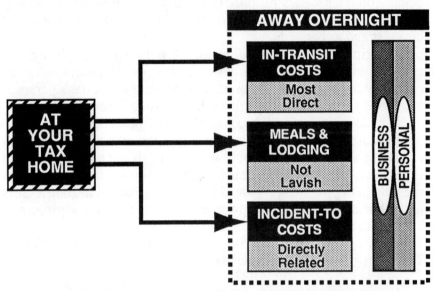

Fig. 5.1 - The Concept of "Segregated Travel Accounting"

The "in-transit" costs are those which you incur from the moment you leave your tax home to the moment you return to it. The only conditions for deductibility are that you must use the most direct commercially available route. Stopovers and round-about routes imply side vacations and visits to family and friends.

Meals and lodging costs in a travel mode are self explanatory, to the extent that they are not "lavish or extravagant under the circumstances" (the statutory wording).

The "incident-to" costs may include small gifts, business-only entertainment, computer software programs, faxing of information between business contacts, laundry and cleaning, special travel accessories, entry fees to business displays, the purchase of business reports and publications, and so on. A "so on" example would be when you arrived at your hotel your luggage was damaged. The luggage repair cost would be "incident-to" your trip.

DEDUCTING JOB EXPENSES

The "Primary Purpose" Rule

When travel expenses include personal activities mixed with business activities, deductibility of the expenditures for business will depend on the *primary purpose* of the trip. The primary purpose is established by the relative amount of time (**in days**) devoted to business and to personal.

If a trip lasted 10 days, for example, and it could be shown that six were bona fide business days, the trip would be construed as primarily for business. If the other way around, six days personal and four days business, the trip would be primarily personal.

Why is this primary purpose distinction important?

Because, if the primary purpose is business, the claimant gets all of his in-transit costs as deductible expense. If the primary purpose is personal, none of the in-transit costs are allowable. Now do you see why in Figure 5.1 we wanted you to segregate all in-transit costs unto themselves, and not group them with meals, lodging, and incident-to expenses?

At this point, we should inform you of Regulation 1.162(b)(1). This subregulation reads in full as follows:

> *If a taxpayer travels to a destination and while at such destination engages in both business and personal activities, traveling expenses **to and from such destination** are deductible only if the trip is related primarily to the taxpayer's trade or business. If the trip is primarily personal in nature, the traveling expenses to and from the destination are not deductible even though the taxpayer engages in business activities while at such destination. However, expenses while **at the destination** which are **properly allocable** to the taxpayer's trade or business are deductible even though the traveling expenses to and from the destination are not deductible.* [Emphasis added.]

The last regulatory sentence above opens up another segregation aspect. The additional segregation requirement is: allocation of time (**in hours**) at the travel destination. This requires a much closer analysis of what constitutes business and personal during an ordinary work day at the destination.

TRAVELING EXPENSES

In substance, then, in-transit time is not broken down into days and hours. The obvious reason is that, while in transit (to or from), one is not at his business destination, and therefore could not conduct business even if he wanted to. It is the at-destination *days* that determine whether the in-transit costs are deductible or not. It is the at-destination time in *hours* that determines the allocation of meals, lodging, and incident-to expenses between business and personal.

Business/Personal Allocations

As to the allocation of at-destination expenses between business and personal, there is no clear regulation on point. The nearest that we can cite is Regulation 1.162-2(b)(2). Its only pertinent sentence reads—

Whether a trip is related primarily to the taxpayer's trade or business or is primarily personal in nature depends on the facts and circumstances in each case. [Emphasis added.]

Requiring a recitation of "facts and circumstances" is not very quantitative. We need more guidance than this. The next nearest is a series of revenue rulings issued by the IRS (in 1975) addressing the sleep or rest requirement for away overnight. The gist of these rulings as interpreted by the Tax Court [*M.L. Johnson*, TC Memo 1982-2] is that—

A taxpayer is traveling away from home if his duties require him to be away from the general area of his tax home for a period substantially longer than an ordinary day's work and, during his time off while away, he needs to get sleep or rest to meet the demands of his work.

For domestic travel, an ordinary day's work consists of eight hours in a 24-hour period. During the 16 hours of nonwork time, there is the "sleep or rest" requirement. This is the lodging part of travel: typically eight hours or so. This leaves eight hours of nonwork, nonlodging time. During this time-off period, the traveler

DEDUCTING JOB EXPENSES

is expected to eat three meals and engage in incidental activities in preparation for the next 8-hour work day.

In other words, in a 24-hour cycle, there are eight hours of work time and 16 hours of off time. It is only the eight hours of work time that are allocable to business and personal. The 16 hours of off time are "free time." They are *not* allocable! They are neither business time nor personal time. If anything, they are meals and lodging time.

Simple 8-Hour Example

The eight hours of accounting-for time at one's business destination applies only to domestic travel. It does **not** apply to foreign travel (which we'll get to later). Domestic travel is that which is within and contiguous to the United States. This includes Canada, Mexico, Alaska, and Hawaii.

Domestically, it is just the 8-hour work period that "facts and circumstances" must be used for business/personal allocations.

Suppose, for example, that during a given travel workday, five hours were spent on bona fide business matters, and three hours on personal matters. For the in-transit primary purpose test, this would be a business day (more than 50%). For the at-destination meals and lodging allocation test, 5/8ths would be business, and 3/8ths would be personal.

Instead of spending three hours of the workday on personal matters, suppose our traveler went back to his lodging room immediately after his five business hours. He made a few business notes, entered a few expenditures in his travel diary, and then rested for the rest of those three hours. Are these three hours personal?

No, they are not. They are on-call business hours. He was available for work, but no work demands were placed upon him. Thus, even though he worked only five hours, he gets credit for a full 8-hour business day.

After the 8-hour workday, our traveler buys an alcoholic drink or two. Afterwards he purchases a theater ticket and goes to a show. Do any of these expenditures qualify as meals and lodging? They were incurred during meals and lodging time, were they not?

TRAVELING EXPENSES

Neither of the two expenditures (alcoholic beverage and theater ticket) qualifies as meals and lodging. The allowance of meals during travel is for the sole purpose of body nourishment and the sustenance of life. Coffee, milk, tea, and water would qualify as food, but not alcohol. The allowance of lodging is for sleep and rest: not for going to the theater.

Let's extend domestic meals and lodging time of a single day to weekend days and holidays. Are weekend days and holidays subject to business/personal allocation rules of "an ordinary day's work"?

No, they are not. Again, we are addressing meals and lodging time whether on weekends, holidays, or after work hours. Except for expenditures for bona fide body nourishment (food) and sleep (or rest), no other expenditures during these times qualify as traveling expenses. The only exceptions are incident-to direct-business items which are segregated unto their own.

Here's a weekend twist that often arises. The business purpose of the trip ends on Friday, after an essentially full workday. The traveler stays over the weekend, sightsees, then returns home on the following Monday. Is the Saturday-Sunday stayover business travel time?

Definitely not. The traveler stayed over for personal reasons. In this case, each weekend day counts as a personal day for allocation purposes.

In other words, weekends (and holidays) count as part of the business trip only if one is required to stay at his business destination (or go to another) in order to continue his business activities the following regular workday.

10-Day Allocation Example

With the above as background, let us go through a comprehensive example for a 10-day domestic business trip. Our traveler departs from his tax home and arrives at his business destination on a Tuesday. That is, Day 1 is an in-transit day. Days 2 through 9 are work-related days. Day 10 (Thursday) is an in-transit day from the business destination back to his tax home. Be mindful that Days 2 through 9 span a normal weekend. Because

DEDUCTING JOB EXPENSES

our traveler's first post-weekend day is a workday, staying there over the weekend is presumed to be business necessitated.

Let us assume that our traveler is reasonably conscientious. He keeps a good travel diary of his ordinary workdays, taking special care to record his business hours, on-call hours, and personal hours.

Using this scenario, a 10-day illustrative travel period is recapitulated in Figure 5.2. As you glance over this table, be aware that on-call time is what is left in an 8-hour day after subtracting the business hours and personal hours for that day. On-call time is treated as business time for travel allocation purposes.

Trip Day	Work Day Hours			Total Hours Account-able	Assigned Days	
	Business	On-Call	Personal		Business	Personal
1 (Tues)	In-Transit			0	-	-
2 (Wed)	6	2	0	8	1	-
3 (Thu)	4	0	4	8	1/2	1/2
4 (Fri)	5	0	3	8	1	0
5 (Sat)	-	-	-	0	1	0
6 (Sun)	-	-	-	0	1	0
7 (Mon)	6	2	0	8	1	0
8 (Tues)	0	2	6	8	0	1
9 (Wed)	5	0	3	8	1	0
10 (Thu)	In-Transit			0	-	-
TOTALS	26	6	16	48	6 1/2	1 1/2

Fig. 5.2 - Allocation Example of a 10-Day Domestic Business Trip

From the results in Figure 5.2, is the trip primarily business or primarily personal?

Of course it is primarily business because that's the way we set it up. Out of the total eight days at destination, 6^1/2 are business and

TRAVELING EXPENSES

1 1/2 are personal. This means that all in-transit costs are tax deductible.

The next question is: for the 48 at-destination accountable hours, what is proper allocation between business and personal time?

As illustrated in Figure 5.2, the business time is 26 hours (actual) plus six hours (on call) for a total of 32 hours. Therefore, the allocation percentage is 32/48 or 66.67%. This is the fraction that you apply to *all* meals and lodging for the 8-day stay at the business destination. This includes the weekend.

Two or More Destinations

If a traveler has one tax home, and visits two or more domestic destinations in the same trip, the *characterization rule* comes into play. That is, each destination must be separately characterized in terms of its primary purpose. Just because the first destination is purely business, all other destinations are not characterized as such, automatically.

Let us exemplify the variety of primary purposes by a 10-destination trip.

Destination 1 is direct business. The customer is unhappy with the product or service of the traveler's trade or business, and the trip was necessary to correct — or commit to correcting — the problem. Had the trip not been taken, the traveler would have lost that customer's business. This is clearly an "ordinary and necessary" travel expense.

Now, for nine other destinations. Is each destination "ordinary and necessary" in the traveler's trade or business?

Destination 2 is contact with a potentially new customer, based on the referral of an old customer. Destination 3 is a chance visit to a competitor's customer. Destination 4 is a random search for new products or services to augment the traveler's existing line of products or services. Destination 5 is a sight-seeing trip en route to Destination 6, which is a business convention and trade show. Destination 7 is a professional conference and seminar. Destination 8 is a 3-day crash course in business accounting. Destination 9 is a stockholders' meeting in which the traveler is a substantial investor.

DEDUCTING JOB EXPENSES

Destination 10 is a company-paid vacation trip to a resort area where other company employees also are in attendance.

With such a variety of destinations, can't you see the tax importance of characterizing each one as a separate and distinct travel purpose of its own?

This is where Regulation 1.162-2(d) comes in. This regulation: *Characterization by facts and circumstances*, reads in full as—

> *Expenses paid or incurred by a taxpayer in attending a convention or other meeting may constitute an ordinary and necessary business expense under section 162 depending upon the facts and circumstances of each case. No distinction will be made between self-employed persons and employees. The fact that an employee uses vacation or leave time or that his attendance at the convention is voluntary will not necessarily prohibit the allowance of the deduction. The allowance of deductions for such expenses will depend on whether there is a **sufficient relationship** between the taxpayer's trade or business and his attendance at the convention or other meeting so that he is **benefiting or advancing** the interests of his trade or business by such attendance. If the convention is for political, social, or other purposes unrelated to the taxpayer's trade or business, the expenses are not deductible.* [Emphasis added.]

The phrase "convention or other meeting" used above is an umbrella for characterizing all destinations which imply a business tone, but which may not be directly related to a business purpose. To help you appreciate the importance of this characterizing-each-destination rule, we present Figure 5.3. Do note that there is a vast "grey area" between purely business travel [Sec. 162(a)] and purely personal travel [Sec. 262(a): Personal, Living, and Family Expenses].

Foreign Travel Accounting

Foreign travel is that which takes place *outside* of the U.S., Canada, and Mexico. It is the total number of days outside,

TRAVELING EXPENSES

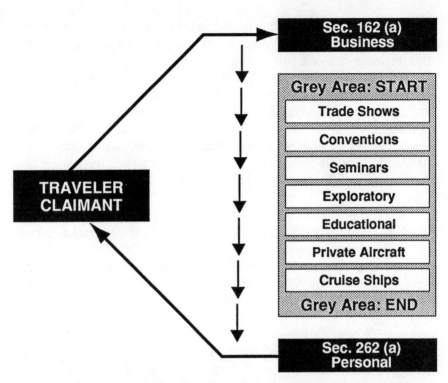

Fig. 5.3 - The "Grey Area" Between Business and Personal Travel

counting travel time as well as lodging time. This differs from domestic travel, where travel time is not counted.

Travel outside starts from a point of departure within the U.S., and ends at a point of arrival back in the U.S. From one's tax home to his U.S. departure point is domestic travel, as is travel from one's U.S. arrival point back to his tax home. The tax rules on these domestic travel legs of a foreign trip are unaffected by the tax rules when outside the U.S.

The tax rules for allocating the business/nonbusiness aspects of foreign travel differ materially from those for domestic travel. The principal reason for the differences is the generally longer travel times involved, the "inefficiencies" in foreign business transactions, and the greater costs and more diverse incidental expenditures required.

DEDUCTING JOB EXPENSES

For tax deduction purposes, the unit of foreign travel accounting is days: not hours. There are no half-days. The count is either a full business day or a full nonbusiness day.

A "day" in foreign travel status is a local time zone day. If you are traveling east, your first outside day is less than 24 hours. If you are traveling west, your first outside day is more than 24 hours. As you already know, the world is divided into 24 standard time zones. Each zone is 15 degrees apart in longitude, starting at Greenwich, England. Not all foreign countries recognize the Greenwich time zone system. Therefore you have to rely on local days — whatever they are — for your counting system.

We stress again that only days are counted: not hours. Using the day-counting method, your total days outside of the U.S. consist of: (1) business days and, (2) nonbusiness days. There are no "mixed-use" days: part business, part personal. Each day (irrespective of the hours spent) is characterized by the principal objective accomplished, or intended to be accomplished, for that day. Unless specifically business, an outside-the-U.S. day is automatically nonbusiness.

A short primer on the methodology for counting foreign travel days is presented in Figure 5.4. Note that if one heads towards a nonbusiness destination before arriving at his business destination, that leg counts as a nonbusiness day.

The "Business Necessity" Test

The fundamental difference between domestic and foreign travel is the business necessity test for foreign travel. If you must go to a foreign destination for unequivocal business reasons, and you indeed attend a business meeting there, you get credit for a full business day. You get full credit even though you may spend only one hour of the day on business. This means that every foreign destination point, separately, must meet the business necessity test. Otherwise, it is counted as a full nonbusiness day and disallowed.

The business necessity test arises from the partial disallowance rule of Section 274(c): *Certain foreign travel*. Paragraph (1) of this rule reads in full as—

TRAVELING EXPENSES

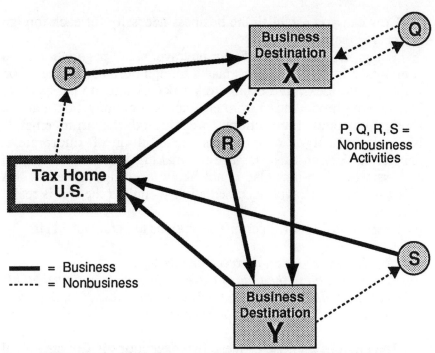

Fig. 5.4 - Counting Foreign Travel Days: Business & Nonbusiness

*In the case of any individual who travels outside of the United States away from home **in pursuit of** a trade or business or in pursuit of an activity described in section 212, **no deduction shall be allowed** under section 162 or section 212 **for that portion of the expenses** of such travel otherwise allowable under such section **which**, under regulations prescribed by the [IRS], **is not allocable** to such trade or business or to such activity.* [Emphasis added.]

The practical effect of the above is that all foreign travel expenses are presumptively disallowed, except to the extent they are "allocable" . . . to Section 162 or Section 212. Section 162, recall, pertains to trade or business expenses, whereas Section 212 pertains to expenses for the production of income. The fact that one must be "in pursuit of" these activities means that the trip must fulfill a business necessity.

DEDUCTING JOB EXPENSES

How can you establish the business necessity for each foreign destination that you visit?

You produce evidence of your pretravel plans, negotiations, and communications. One doesn't take a foreign business trip based on whims, good ideas, and exploratory risks. There are passports to update, emigration and custom clearances, immunization matters, foreign currency transactions, prepaid lodging arrangements, international flight connections, scheduling of interpreters, contacting foreign business agents, making inquiries to foreign embassies, and so on. One is not likely to go through all of this effort — with pretravel documentation — unless the trip is really necessary.

Subsection 274(c)(2) permits exceptions to paragraph (1) if—

(A) such travel does not exceed one week, or
(B) the portion of the time of travel . . . which is not attributable to the pursuit of the taxpayer's trade or business . . . is less than 25 percent of the total time on such travel.

The obvious purpose of these two exceptions is Congressional recognition of life in the real world. To disqualify a business day due solely to some incidental opportunistic, nonbusiness activity, is interpretive harshness in the extreme. Unfortunately, though, many IRS agents do not comprehend the significance of these exceptions. They still expect a strict accounting of the business/nonbusiness days . . . for all foreign travel.

En Route "Allocation" Required

The whole purpose of counting the business/nonbusiness days of foreign travel is to establish an *allocation fraction* (or percentage) for en route expenditures. The allocation fraction is that figure which results when dividing the number of business days by the total number of days (business plus nonbusiness) outside the U.S. For example, if there were 23 days outside, of which 15 were business days, the allocation fraction would be—

$15/23 = 0.6522$, or 65.22%

TRAVELING EXPENSES

The allocation process applies to each foreign trip separately on its own. Where there is more than one business destination on a given trip, there may be several en route "legs." All of the en route legs are added together for each trip, for allocation purposes.

For proper allocation, one must first sort out the *qualified* en route expenses. These are those expenses required by the most reasonably direct route in getting to your first business destination, traveling between business destinations, and getting back to the United States.

The most obvious en route expenses are transportation costs, whether by air, land, or water. But in foreign travel, particularly en route, costs may also include necessary food and rest . . . *while in transit.* International travel is fraught with hangups, holdups, misconnections, and layovers. If these matters require expenditures for food and rest, which are not included in the transit fare, they become qualified en route expenses.

Disqualified en route expenses are those which are incurred for side trips, vacation hops, seeing friends, and roundabout routes where scheduled layovers become tourist opportunities. None of these expenses qualify. Taxwise, they are disallowed in full. If included in the qualified expenses, they must be excluded.

To illustrate the en route allocation process, let's take a very simple example. Consider that the total en route expenditures for a 23-day trip amount to $12,860. Of this amount, we can identify $8,930 as being qualified and $3,750 as being nonqualified. It is the $8,930 figure to which the day-counting allocation fraction applies. Assume that there were 15 business days.

Using the 15/23 allocation fraction (namely: 0.6522), the deductible en route expenses become:

$8,930 x 0.6522 = $5,824.

Can you see what has happened?

Even though we can isolate $8,930 as qualified en route expenses, we are penalized by the eight nonbusiness days (15 + 8 = 23). The rationale is that the nonbusiness days benefited from the business days counting method. This is the bottom line significance

DEDUCTING JOB EXPENSES

of the partial disallowance (allocation) rule of Section 274(c)(1), quoted in full above.

A Realistic Example

Let us present a realistic example in a way that portrays the various subtleties of the foreign travel rules.

As a Section 162 business person, you fly from San Francisco to New York, and spend two days there on business. This leg of your trip costs you $850 (travel, meals, and lodging). You depart New York and fly to Riyadh, Saudi Arabia where you spend 15 days on business. It takes you 1-1/2 days to get there, at a cost of $1,650. Your 15 days in Riyadh cost you $3,200 (meals and lodging mostly). You leave Riyadh and fly to London (1 day) and spend 10 days touring England. Your flight to London costs you $1,450, and the tour of England costs you $1,860. You return to San Francisco from London (1 day) flying over the polar route. The fare from London to San Francisco costs you $1,750.

What are your tax deductible travel expenses? What are your nondeductible expenses?

We pictorialize this example in Figure 5.5. Obviously, our sketch is not to scale. We just want to use it to highlight the tax principles involved.

The domestic travel from San Francisco to New York, and the two days there are fully deductible. You exclude, of course — as always — any personal entertainment in New York. Otherwise, this portion of your trip is 100% business. The number of days involved are not counted in your foreign travel allocation.

The total number of days that you spend outside of the U.S. is 29 days. We recap this number as follows:

	Days		Cost
New York to Riyadh	2	(B)	$ 2,650
Business in Riyadh	15	(B)	3,200
Riyadh to London	1	(NB)	1,450
Vacation in England	10	(NB)	1,860
London to San Francisco	1	(B)	1,750
Total	29 days		$10,910

TRAVELING EXPENSES

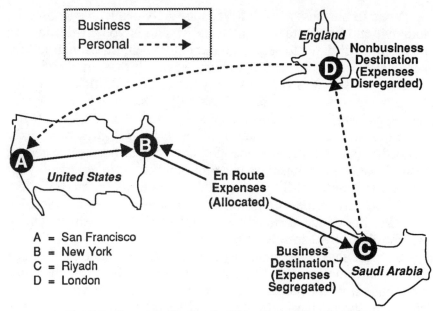

Fig. 5.5 - Example: En Route Allocation of Foreign Trip

The number of business days (indicated by each letter "B" above) that you spent outside of the U.S. is 18 days. This means that your en route costs to and from Riyadh (your foreign business destination) are allowable to the extent of 18/29th (or 62.06%).

Since you did not return directly home from Riyadh, your business-destination en route cost is two times the fare from New York to Riyadh (2,650 x 2 = $5,300). Your actual total fare was 2,650 + 1,450 + 1,750 = $5,850. The extra $550 (5,850 – 5,300) that it cost you to fly home via London is a purely personal expense: nondeductible, nonallocable.

From the foregoing tabulation of days, you spent 11 nonbusiness ("NB") days outside the U.S. This is more than 25% personal time: 11/29 = 37.93%. This means that the allocation exception of Section 274(c)(2)(B) does not apply. Hence your en route business-travel costs of $5,300 are "allocated" as follows:

Deductible portion: $5,300 x 18/29 = 3,290
Nondeductible portion: $5,300 x 11/29 = <u>2,010</u>
                                                                  $5,300

DEDUCTING JOB EXPENSES

Your 15 business days in Riyadh are fully deductible (for meals, lodging, and incidentals). But since Riyadh is your at-destination point, you still have to segregate out any expenditures incurred for personal pleasure, recreation, or sightseeing. If they are de minimis in amount, say less than 5% of your total at-destination costs, segregation is not required. These small personal expenditures are treated as "working condition" fringe benefits [Sec. 132(a)(3), (4)].

Your 10 days of vacation in England are obviously nondeductible. But if you attended any type of business meeting, visited one or more business locations, and/or made reports to your home office in the U.S., your out-of-pocket costs for these matters would be deductible. Quite often, a business traveler on foreign vacation does indeed incur incidental business expenses which, when isolated by themselves, are deductible.

Suppose that, when planning the Riyadh trip, the leg to London was intentionally included for contingency business reasons. London is a well-established international hub for ready access to Northern Europe, the Baltic states, and Scandinavia. As an alternate business route, a traveler could go to London to stand by for further orders from his home office. Through diplimatic channels, the home office could be arranging for new business contacts in those European and East European countries readily accessible from London.

In such a case, if it can be shown that the trip to London from Riyadh was not undertaken with vacation foremost in mind, the London travel leg (en route) would qualify as a business day.

6

MOVING EXPENSES

> Whether A Job Move Is Domestic Or Foreign, Certain "In Connection With" Expenses Are Tax Allowed. The New Job Must Be At Least 50 Miles Farther Commute Distance Away, And Must Last For At Least 39 Weeks. Deductible Expenses Are: (A) Transportation And Storage Of Household Goods And Personal Effects, And (B) One-Way Travel And Lodging Of You And Household Members. When Claiming These Expenses On Form 3903 (Or 3903-F), Caution Is Required Regarding Employer Reimbursements Which Are NOT Included In Box 1 (Wages, Etc.) Of Your Form W-2.

Moving expenses are those which we characterized as Class IV in Chapter 1. They are those expenditures which are necessary when moving from your personal home to your first tax home (first job), or from one tax home to another tax home (new job). These are expenses for moving you, your family, your household goods, and personal effects. They are allowable only if employment necessitated and incurred **after** being offered a job at the distant work location. They are for permanent moves: not temporary.

Allowable moving expenses are those which are *job necessitated*. This means that you don't move to look for a job. You must get a job, job offer, or job transfer first, then move to fulfill that job. That is, you have to move to fulfill your occupational duties on a continuous and ongoing basis. The justification for allowing moving expenses as a job expense deduction is the fact that you pay income taxes on your new job

DEDUCTING JOB EXPENSES

earnings. Without a job — or promise of one — there is no income and, therefore, no deductible expenses therewith. When applicable, the expenses are allowable whether the move is domestic or foreign.

The allowability of moving expenses is authorized by Section 217 of the IR Code. This section is titled: *Moving Expenses*. We are going to discuss this section quite extensively in this chapter. Certain qualifying conditions must be met, and certain tax forms (namely: Forms 3093 and 3903-F) must be used. There are certain tax-word tricks that the IRS uses to befuddle you, and to distract you from claiming your legitimate deductions. We want you to be alert to these tricks and be prepared to claim your due. Moving expenses are treated as an "adjustment to income" rather than as "miscellaneous deductions" as is the case for job expense Classes I, II, and III. We'll explain this treatment difference as we go along.

At Least 50 Miles

Before any moving expenses are allowable, there is one basic precondition to be met. This is the *distance* test. Stated simply, this distance test is 50 miles or more. But which 50 miles are we talking about? The distance between the old and new tax homes (workplaces)? Or the distance between the old and new personal homes (residences)?

Answer: Neither one.

The 50-mile test is the increase in commuting distance from one's old residence to his new workplace, relative to his old commute distance. In other words, the test is your *increase in commuting distance*, should you choose not to move your personal residence. This increase in distance shall be . . . *the shortest of the more commonly traveled routes*.

Let us illustrate this distance test with simple numbers. Your old commute distance is 15 miles. Your new commute distance (without moving) is 65 miles. It's a simple subtraction, namely:

```
Step 1 — Old residence to new workplace        65 miles
         (New commute distance)
Step 2 — Old residence to old workplace        15 miles
         (Old commute distance)                --------
```

MOVING EXPENSES

Step 3 — Subtract step 2 from step 1   50 miles
         (Increase in commute distance)

The statutory wording on point is set forth in Section 217(c): *Conditions for Allowance.* It reads in part as—

> *No deduction shall be allowed under* [Section 217: Moving expenses] *unless—*
> *(1) the taxpayer's new principal place of work—*
>
> > *(A) is at least 50 miles farther from his residence than was his former principal place of work, or*
> >
> > *(B) if he had no former principal place of work, is at least 50 miles from his former residence.*

If your change in workplace commute distance is on the borderline of 50 miles, you had better do some homework. Carefully measure the distances and routes, and determine which are the shortest and most direct. Then create the backup documentation. Have it certified by a disinterested party (such as a traffic officer or auto association official). The potential moving expense deduction is too substantial to risk its disallowance in a borderline case.

To help you visualize the 50-mile test, we present Figure 6.1. Note that Case A meets the test, whereas Case B does not. Case B usually occurs when a job change takes place within the same metropolitan area.

There is also a proximity requirement when actually moving. Your new residence should be reasonably proximate to your new work location. Regulation 1.217-2(a)(3) points out that—

> *A move is not considered to be reasonably proximate . . . where the distance between the taxpayer's new residence and his new principal place of work exceeds the distance between his former residence and his new principal place of work.*

The idea behind this proximity regulation is that your new residence should be within ordinary commute distance of your new

DEDUCTING JOB EXPENSES

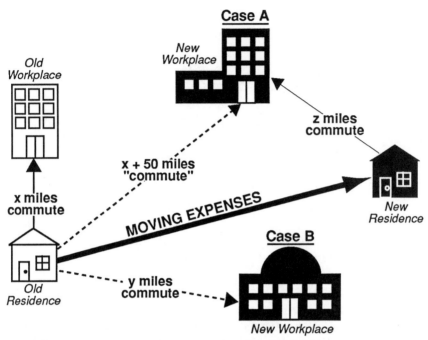

Fig. 6.1 - The "At Least 50 Miles Farther" Moving Expense Test

workplace. The rule-of-thumb is within 50 miles. After all, the whole purpose of the moving expense deduction is to enable you to work proficiently at your new tax home. It is not an opportunity to move to your dreamhouse location, irrespective of distance.

For Commencement of Work

There is another precondition before moving expenses are allowed. This is the commencement-of-work test. The commencement must occur at a new principal place of business. If no new work commences, the move is personal: not business. This precludes any moving expenses to second homes, investment locations, vacation resorts, retirement communities, and leisure worlds. Work *must commence* . . . either before or after the move.

The law on point is Section 217(a): **Deduction Allowed**. This subsection reads—

MOVING EXPENSES

*There shall be allowed as a deduction moving expenses paid or incurred during the taxable year in connection with the **commencement of work** by the taxpayer as an employee ... at a **new principal place of work**.* [Emphasis added.]

Note that there is no condition on the type of employment at the new work location. The inference, of course, is that one must be engaged in the active pursuit of a trade, business, or profession. Engaging in new investment activities is not considered employment of any kind.

The term *commencement* means the starting of work EITHER—

(a) for the first time or after a substantial period of unemployment or part-time employment;
(b) for a different employer, possibly in a new trade or business; or
(c) for the same employer in the same trade or business at a new location.

One must commence his work within a reasonable length of time — either before or after — arriving at his new location. Generally, this period of time is within one year. Regulation 1.217-2(a)(3) specifically says—

In general, moving expenses incurred within 1 year of the date of the commencement of work are considered to be reasonably proximate in time to such commencement.

The cited regulation also accepts extenuating circumstances and good causes for not completing a move within one year of commencement. Family matters (such as schooling, hospitalization, spouse working), and uncertainties over the new job duration, are acceptable reasons for untimely moves.

A new *principal place of work* is where one spends most of his employment time, or where his trade or business activities are centered. Either is usually the place where one reports to work for assignments for a more or less indefinite period of time. If one has

DEDUCTING JOB EXPENSES

two or more jobs at the new location, each at different reporting centers, the job which produces the highest gross income is the "principal" place of work.

Time at New Location

There is still one more (important) precondition that we must tell you about. It is the *minimum time* at new location rule. Unless one stays at his new principal place of employment for at least a specified length of time, all moving expenses associated therewith are disallowed. The obvious purpose of this rule is to discourage a claimant from accepting short, temporary employment, just to get his moving expenses allowed.

There are two parts to the minimum-time rule. One part is for employed persons: called the "39 week" rule. The second part is for self-employed persons: called the "78 week" rule. Both parts are prescribed in Section 217(c)(2): *Conditions for Allowance*: Minimum Time Period(s). We'll skip the 78-week rule. Any addressing of self-employed individuals is beyond the scope of this book.

We quote the 39-week rule in full as follows:

> *No deduction shall be allowed under* [Section 217] *unless—*
> *(A) during the 12-month period immediately following his **arrival** in the general location of his new principal place of work, the taxpayer is a **full-time** employee, in such general location, during **at least 39 weeks**.* [Emphasis added.]

A period of 39 weeks is nine months. Thus, there are three months of "free time" within the 12-month period. This free time is to allow for seasonal adjustments for particular occupations, and for necessary acclimation before commencement of work. The term "arrival" means the date on which the claimant commences his new work on a regular basis. It is not the date that one's family or household goods and effects arrive.

The term "full time" means exclusively available for work during each week of the 39-week qualifying period. One's availability is determined by the customary practices of his

MOVING EXPENSES

occupation. Temporary absences due to illness, strikes, paid vacations, natural disasters, etc. are discounted. They have no effect on the full-time availability concept. Nor does the claimant have to work for the same employer in the same business during the 39-week period.

In a husband and wife situation, where both spouses commence work at the same new location, *either spouse* may satisfy the 39-week test. Thus, if one spouse voluntarily ceases employment (for whatever reason), there is no effect on the qualifying spouse. They may file a joint return and claim all of their joint moving expenses.

There are exceptions to the 39-week minimum full-time rule. They are spelled out in Section 217(d)(1) as—

(i) death or disability, or
(ii) involuntary separation from service (other than for willful misconduct) or transfer for the benefit of an employer.

There is also another exception to the 39-week rule. It is for retirees or survivors of decedents who were working abroad. Qualified "retiree" moving expenses and qualified "survivor" moving expenses are allowable under Section 217(i).

While working abroad, if one qualifies for regular retirement under his employment contract, his moving expenses back to the U.S. are allowed [Sec. 217(i)(1), (2)]. Ordinarily, when one retires from his employment, he is not allowed any expenses for moving to his principal place of retirement. The obvious reason is: he is not "commencing work" there. The obvious reason for allowing a person working abroad to move to his retirement in the U.S. is to avoid forcing him to retire abroad. There are also some jurisdictional tax issues when retiring abroad.

Similarly, for a "qualified survivor" of a worker who becomes deceased while working abroad. A qualified survivor is a spouse or any dependent of a decedent who, at the time of his demise, had his principal place of work outside the U.S. To be allowable, the move back to the U.S. must commence within six months of the death of the decedent worker [Sec. 217(i)(1), (3)]. Then, there is a U.S. death tax return to be prepared by the survivor.

DEDUCTING JOB EXPENSES

"Moving Expenses" Defined

Section 217(b): *Definition of Moving Expenses*, prescribes in full that—

(1) For purposes of [Section 217], *the term "moving expenses" means only the **reasonable expenses**—*
  (A) of moving household goods and personal effects from the former residence to the new residence, and
  (B) of traveling (including lodging) from the former residence to the new place of residence.
Such term shall not include any expenses for meals.

(2) In the case of any individual other than the taxpayer, expenses referred to in paragraph (1) shall be taken into account only if such individual has both the former residence and the new residence as his principal place of abode and is a member of the taxpayer's household.

Regulation 1.217-2(b)(2)(i) defines "reasonable expenses" as those which are—

reasonable under the circumstances of the particular move. Expenses paid or incurred in excess of a reasonable amount are not deductible. Generally, expenses paid or incurred for movement of household goods and personal effects or for travel (including lodging) are reasonable to the extent that they are . . . by the shortest and most direct route available from the former residence to the new residence . . . and in the shortest period of time commonly required to travel the distance involved by such mode. Thus, if moving or travel arrangements are made to provide a circuitous route for scenic, stopover, or other similar reasons, additional expenses resulting therefrom are not deductible since they are not . . . related to the commencement of work at the new principal place of work.

The above regulation goes on to point out that you can deduct all costs of connecting or disconnecting utilities to move, pack, crate,

MOVING EXPENSES

and transport your household goods, appliances, furniture, clothing, and other personal effects. This includes the cost of shipping your car, recreational vehicles, sports equipment, and household pets. Deductible expenses also include the cost of storing and insuring your household goods and personal effects within any period of *30 consecutive days* after the day your things are moved from your former home and before they are delivered to your new home.

Your traveling expenses are limited to those incurred going one way only. That is, you can deduct the cost of transportation and lodging for yourself and members of your household en route from your former home to your new home. This includes lodging expenses in the area of your former home within one day after you could not live in your former home because your furniture had been moved. If you use your own car for the one-way trip, you can deduct your actual en route expenses, or use the standard allowance rate of 9 cents per mile.

There are certain expenses that you cannot deduct as moving expenses. These, together with those that you can deduct, are summarized in Figure 6.2. For all deductible expenses, you are expected to keep accurate records of the items involved. You'll need these records for preparing your tax return for the year of the move.

Use of Form 3903 or 3903-F

To claim deduction for moving expenses, you must prepare Form 3903 (or 3903-F) and attach it to Form 1040. Form 3903 is titled: ***Moving Expenses***; Form 3903-F is titled: ***Foreign Moving Expenses***. Except for the distance requirement for domestic moves, the two forms are identical. Each has the same two expense entry lines, namely:

A. *Transportation and storage of household goods and personal effects.*
B. *Travel and lodging expenses of moving from your old home to your new home.* ***Do not*** *include meals.*

As for the distance test for domestic moves, Form 3903 requires that it be: ***at least 50 miles***, as explained earlier.

DEDUCTING JOB EXPENSES

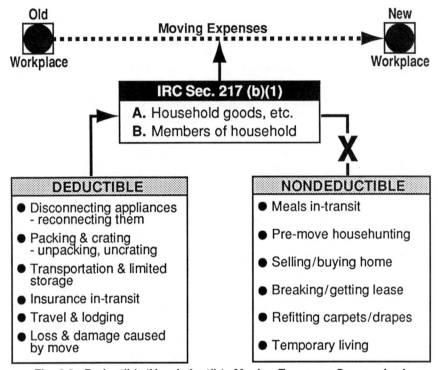

Fig. 6.2 - Deductible/Nondeductible Moving Expenses Summarized

As to Form 3903-F, the domestic distance test is replaced with—

1. *City and country in which your **old workplace** was located*   ▶ ....

2. *City and country in which your **new workplace** is located*   ▶ ....

It would be rare indeed for any foreign move to be less than 50 miles. Hence, specific distances are not required on Form 3903-F.

Just below the new-workplace entry lines, both forms display the admonition:

*See **Time Test** in the instructions.*

MOVING EXPENSES

This is that 39-week rule we mentioned above. It applies to both forms. The only time difference between the two forms is the in-transit storage time. Whereas only 30 days' storage is allowed in domestic moves, for foreign moves, storage is allowable for all of the time that your new job location is outside of the U.S.

Reimbursement Precautions

An edited/abridged version of Form 3903 (or 3903-F) is presented in Figure 6.3. Note the two primary expense entry lines, A and B. The full official wording on these lines was cited earlier. We have simply abbreviated this wording in Figure 6.3. Line C is self-explanatory: *Add lines A and B.* It is Line D that we particularly want to call to your attention. This is where all of the confusion arises, and where the IRS plays its word-twisting tricks on you.

We have identified Line D in Figure 6.3 as: "Amount of employer reimbursement NOT in Box 1 of Form W-2." This is an oversimplification. The full official wording at Line D reads—

> *Enter the total amount your employer paid for your move (including the value of services furnished in kind) that is **not** included in the wages box (Box 1) of your W-2 form. This amount should be identified with Code **P** in Box 13 of your W-2 form.*

This official wording is not very clear. To understand it, you have to understand the tricks of the IRS.

Back in Chapter 2: Scrutinizing Form W-2, we warned you that the IRS is constantly beating on and hounding employers to include every conceivable form of compensation possible in Box 1 of your W-2. If you will recall, this box is titled: *Wages, tips, other compensation.* By insisting that your employer pack this box with every fringe benefit and expense reimbursement to you, the IRS allows your employer to claim these amounts as **his** business expenses. It is then up to you to claim your own business/moving expenses by "backing them out" of Box 1.

DEDUCTING JOB EXPENSES

Form 3903	MOVING EXPENSES	Form 3903 - F
Distance Requirement: ☐ Old ☐ New Domestic Moves		City and Country: ☐ Old ☐ New Foreign Moves

A	Transportation and storage of household goods and personal effects ▶	
B	Travel and lodging expenses of moving from old home to new home. Do not include meals ▶	
C	Add **A** and **B** ·············▶	☐
D	Amount of employer reimbursement, NOT in Box 1 of Form W-2	

• Is **C** more than **D** ?

Yes ▶ you have deductible expenses

No ▶ you have includible excess reimbursements

See text. Also see instructions on official form.

Fig. 6.3 - Edited and Abridged Version of Moving Expenses Form

At this point, please go back and reread the official wording above. Focus on the phrase that reads—

*... that is **not** included in the wages box of your W-2 form.*

In other words, if you received any reimbursement for your moving expenses, and that reimbursement amount **is** included in Box 1 of your W-2, DO NOT ENTER said amount on Line D of Form 3903 (or 3903-F). If you do, you wind up paying tax **twice** on your reimbursed amount. You pay it on the Box 1 amount and you pay it again by erroneously reducing your Line C amount.

MOVING EXPENSES

How do you know whether — and how much — moving expense reimbursement is included in Box 1 (of your W-2 form)?

Answer: Ask your employer. In fact, request that he give you a written statement of the precise amount included. If, because of the move, there are communication difficulties between you and your employer, *assume* the worst. Assume that all of your moving expenses *are* included in Box 1 of your W-2 form, then leave Line D blank (or enter "zero"). This way, you'll be sure of staking maximum claim to all of your bona fide moving expenses.

Meaning of "Code P"

Once again, the second sentence to the official instruction at Line D (in Figure 6.3) reads—

This amount should be identified with Code P in Box 13 of your W-2 form.

The term "this amount" refers to the amount of reimbursement that is NOT included in Box 1 of your W-2. The amount identified as Code P in Box 13 is the amount you enter on Line D, if you want to claim any A or B expenses which are over and above the amount for which you have been reimbursed.

Suppose, for example, your combined A and B expenditures totaled $13,683. Your employer Code P reimbursed you for $12,000. Obviously, your excess expenditures would be $1,683 (13,683 − 12,000). BUT, in order to claim this excess amount on Form 3903, you enter the full $13,683 amount on Line C, and the full $12,000 amount on Line D. When you subtract Line D from Line C, you enter the $1,683 amount on the very last line on Form 3903 (not shown in Figure 6.3). This net amount — excess of reimbursement — becomes your allowable moving expense deduction.

The Code P amount is identified in the "Notice to Employee" on your W-2 as—

Excludable moving expense reimbursement.

DEDUCTING JOB EXPENSES

This means that your employer is instructed to treat the Code P amount as—

> *an excludable fringe benefit . . . not subject to withholding, social security, or medicare taxes.*

What If Excess Reimbursement?

There is a constructive rationale to the Code P reimbursement process. It is premised on *mutual accountability* between employer and employee. The employee reports the true amount expended, with documents and receipts. The employer, in turn, reimburses the employee for the full amount documented. The expenditures and reimbursements are "even steven." There are no excess expenditures; there are no excess reimbursements. The employer does not report the amount as Box 1 wages; the employee does not claim the amount as Form 3903 expenses. The Code P arrangement saves paperwork all around.

But, in most cases, moving oneself and his family to a new work location is a disruption to ordinary living. Many expenses are incurred which are over and above those which are recognized as deductible under Section 217. Often, therefore, many employers will "sweeten the deal." They pay out money to the employee for in-kind services, which exceeds the tax deductible amount. What happens when reimbursement exceeds allowable expenses?

Answer: The excess reimbursement winds up as taxable income on the *Wages* line on page 1 of Form 1040. There is a preprinted instructional directive to this effect on both Forms 3903 and 3903-F. It appears at your "No" answer to the Figure 6.3 question: "Is C greater than D?" If not, you are told—

> *You **cannot** deduct your moving expenses. [Instead], subtract C from D and include the result in income on Form 1040.*

7

BUSINESS USE OF AUTO

> If You Buy Or Lease A Passenger Auto, And Use It For Business Purposes, You MUST Keep A Business Mileage Diary To Establish Your "Business Use Percentage" (BUP). The BUP Applies Across The Board To All Buying, Leasing, And Operating Expenses: Gas, Oil, Repairs, Maintenance, Tires, Insurance, Etc. Allowable Depreciation Of Purchased Autos Is Limited To Less Than $15,000 Over A 5-Year Period. Use Of The "Standard Mileage Rate" Can Avoid Some Recordkeeping. Another Option Is To Lease An Auto, But This Requires A SUBTRACTION Amount From Your Lease Payments. Employer-Provided Autos Are Treated As "Taxable Fringe Benefits."

By far, a passenger automobile is the most widely used item for job-related business purposes. This includes any light truck or van which is fitted primarily for passenger transport, rather than for the transport of equipment and materials. Where a driver and passengers are involved, the course of transport is over public highways, streets, and roads. It is the use of these public facilities that makes the passenger auto a convenient and flexible business tool.

Except in highly congested metropolitan areas, the business use of a passenger auto is indispensable. Indeed, it is difficult to visualize any employment activity where, at least some time during the year, an auto is not used for face-to-face contact in a business transaction.

DEDUCTING JOB EXPENSES

The negative side of every passenger auto is its passenger-carrying capability. This gives it an adverse tax implication. A passenger may be the employee claimant's spouse, a member of his family, a friend, or other person or persons who are not essential to the business use of the vehicle. This possibility enables the IRS to assert that no such vehicle can ever be 100% pure business. On this assertion alone, stringent rules and procedures have been established to restrict the allowable expense deduction for business use of an auto . . . whether employee-owned (or leased) or employer-owned (or leased).

The stringency of the tax rules on the business use of autos is based on the premise that there are two distinct classes involved. There are economy autos (costing less than $15,000) and there are luxury autos (costing more than $15,000). This distinction arises because of the limitation on cost recovery for depreciation imposed by Section 280F: *Limitation on Depreciation for Luxury Automobiles*. When you add up the five years of cost recovery depreciation limits, you arrive at a cost figure of under $15,000.

This and certain other fundamentals you should know about when using any passenger auto for business and job purposes.

Classed as "Listed Property"

Leave it to the IRS to come up with a buzz phrase to stop you cold, before claiming any business use of a passenger auto. The buzz phrase is: *Listed Property*. What does this mean?

It means that, before you claim any business deduction for your auto usage, you have to answer certain checkbox questions on your tax forms. The questions are designed to warn you about he substantiation requirements that you must meet. There are four of these questions, which we have edited slightly:

1. *Do you have evidence to support the business use claimed?*
 ☐ Yes ☐ No

2. *If "Yes," is the evidence written?* ☐ Yes ☐ No

BUSINESS USE OF AUTO

3. *Is another vehicle available for personal use?*
   ☐ *Yes* ☐ *No*

4. *If employer provided, was personal use of vehicle permitted during off-duty hours?* ☐ *Yes* ☐ *No*

Obviously, if you answer "No" to any of these questions, you'll have a rough time claiming business use of your auto. You may still have a rough time even when answering "Yes" to all questions. You would be expected to prove your "Yeses."

The above questions on the tax forms are an outgrowth of Section 274(d) regarding travel substantiation requirements. The portion pertinent to passenger automobiles is—

No deduction ... shall be allowed ... with respect to any listed property (as defined in section 280F(d)(4)), unless the taxpayer substantiates by adequate records or by sufficient evidence ...

When you look at Section 280F(d)(4), you will find that—

The term "listed property" means—
(i)   any passenger automobile, [and]
(ii) any other [vehicle] used as a means of transportation.

Elsewhere in Section 280F(d), you'll find that a passenger auto is any 4-wheeled vehicle, weighing 6,000 pounds or less, manufactured primarily for use on public streets, roads, and highways. The term also includes any part, component, or other item that is attached to the automobile or is traditionally included in its purchase price.

Thus, by classifying an automobile as listed property, there is a statutory guarantee against your being able to claim 100% business use of it.

Business Use Percentage

Since you cannot claim 100% business use of a passenger auto, what can you claim? If you substantiate your business usage

DEDUCTING JOB EXPENSES

properly, you can claim whatever business use percentage that you can establish. That is, with proof, you can claim 90%, 65%, 50%, 35% . . . or whatever. The percentage you establish is applied to all operating expenses (gas, oil, repairs, car washes), to all ownership expenses (registration, interest, insurance, extended warranties) to the statutory depreciation allowance (if owned), and to lease and rental payments (with statutory inclusion amounts).

If you own or lease two or more autos and use each in business, you must establish a separate business use percentage for each vehicle. You cannot combine the two or more usages and apply them to the one vehicle that gives you the best tax writeoffs.

For a given auto, for a given taxable year, you need to establish your total business mileage for that year. You need also to establish the total miles driven (business and nonbusiness) for the subject year. With this data, your business use percentage (BUP) becomes—

$$\text{BUP} = \frac{\text{Total business miles}}{\text{Total miles: business and nonbusiness}} = \underline{}\%$$

Your BUP is rarely the same percentage figure year after year. It will vary depending on each year's business operations. Consequently, you have to compute a different percentage each year. Once computed for a given year, your BUP applies across-the-board to your total auto expenses: business and nonbusiness alike. This means that during the year you do not have to segregate business from nonbusiness. The BUP takes care of this segregation at the end of the taxable year.

Log All Business Trips

As owner/buyer (or leasee) of a passenger auto used for job purposes. your very first recordkeeping chore is to prepare and maintain a *business mileage log*. Furthermore, the log should be "regularly posted." There should be a separate mileage log for each vehicle used. As stated previously, your total business mileage on each vehicle is a prerequisite for establishing its BUP.

The term "regularly posted" means no less frequently than once a week. Postings daily — or upon completion of each business trip

BUSINESS USE OF AUTO

— are preferable. In other words, a business mileage diary. It should be an entirely separate document of its own. We know this sounds tedious and boring but, once you get in the habit, it is not all that bad. Trust us. A timely prepared mileage log will truly work magic when — NOT "if" — your auto expenses are challenged by the IRS. It's the very first auto item the IRS asks for.

Your mileage diary should be designed in such a way that each day of the week is displayed with ample space. As the business user, you want to have enough room to enter each destination and its mileage (one-way or round-trip, as applicable) from your tax home. If there is more than one business trip in a given day, make the mileage distinction clear. Technically, each trip should have a distinct purpose of its own. In some specific way, each trip should relate to your trade, business, or income-producing activity.

In the front of your business mileage log, we suggest reserving one page for entering odometer readings, at the beginning and ending of the year. You will need the total miles driven (business *and* nonbusiness) — from January 1 through December 31 — for computing your business use percentage.

At the back of your mileage log, we suggest using several pages for recording all operating expenses throughout the year. Designate separate columns for (a) gas and oil, (b) repairs and maintenance, (c) car washes, (d) parking and tolls, (e) tires and parts, and so on. Make the entries as they occur, and date them. Staple your repair invoices and other receipts to the very last page of your diary.

As to the main mileage-logging portion of your diary, there should be space at the end of each month for subtotaling all business miles for that month. An entry at the lower right-hand corner would be ideal. At the end of the year, you add up the 12 subtotals. This constitutes your total business mileage for the year. Divide this number by the total business plus nonbusiness mileage for the year (the difference in those odometer readings in the front of your diary), and you come up with the BUP for that vehicle.

To help you visualize the ideal format of a business mileage log, we present Figure 7.1. You can design such a diary yourself to fit your own needs, or you can buy adaptable diaries from office supply and stationery stores. They should be of pocket size: something you can stick in the glove compartment of your auto or

DEDUCTING JOB EXPENSES

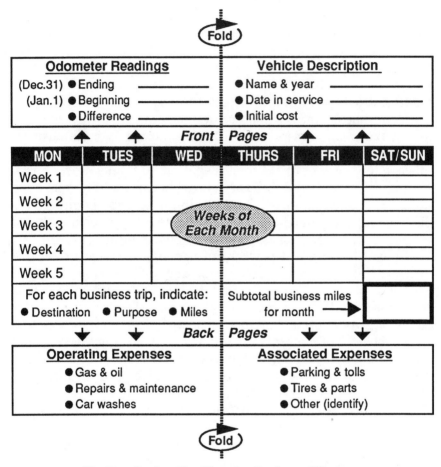

Fig. 7.1 - Pocket-Size Diary for Business Mileage

in the breast pocket of your coat or shirt. It might also be convenient to attach to the diary a road map with your most frequently visited business designations identified thereon.

Verifying Odometer Readings

Do note in Figure 7.1 that we show the odometer reading as: *Ending* and *Beginning* . . . for the business travel year. We show the ending reading first (namely, December 31) because that will be a higher number than the beginning reading on January 1. Then we

BUSINESS USE OF AUTO

show space for entering the difference between the two. You look at your odometer each year end and record the readings yourself.

Since you record the readings, how can you prove their accuracy to a skeptical tax agent, some two or three years later?

It is not as difficult as you might think. You need some "third-party" odometer recordings in the early part of the year **and** in the latter part of the year. By early in the year, we mean within the first three months; by later in the year, we mean the last three months.

The most likely odometer documents are *repair and servicing invoices*. Most such invoices have a box-section for entering the odometer reading, and another box or line for entering the date. The dealer doing the repairs to or servicing of your auto has no interest in your tax affairs. So, if he writes in an odometer reading on a preprinted billing invoice (and there is no evidence of any alteration thereto), that reading is accepted as prima facie fact.

It then becomes a matter of taking the two third-party readings, determining the difference, and figuring the number of elapsed days in between. You then "annualize" the mileage on a 365-day basis. The computed total (business plus nonbusiness) mileage should come pretty close to your own readings.

If your preventive maintenance schedule is not normally near the beginning or ending of the year, perhaps you could arrange to have some minor repair made, just to get a bona fide billing invoice with an odometer recording thereon.

For example, suppose you had some minor repairs made to your auto on March 10th. Your odometer read 18,192 miles. On November 25th, you had a lube and service job on the same vehicle. Your odometer then read 30,684 miles The difference is 30,684 minus 18,192 equals 12,942 miles. The number of days between March 10th and November 25th is 260 days. By annualizing, the total miles driven for the year become—

$$\frac{12{,}942 \text{ miles}}{260 \text{ days}} \times 365 \text{ days/year} = 18{,}168 \text{ miles.}$$

If your self-recorded total mileage is within plus or minus 10% of the annualized total — say between 16,500 and 19,500 — your figure would most likely be accepted as correct.

DEDUCTING JOB EXPENSES

Mileage Entries on Form 2106

Why are we stressing odometer readings and mileage logs so much? Because this is THE KEY to being allowed to deduct all auto expenses that are related to the performance of your job as an employee. Also, it is because **Form 2106**: *Employee Business Expenses* [Part II: Vehicle Expenses] requires specific mileage entries. These mileage entries cannot be "guessed at" or approximated. They must be based on written or other corroborative evidence of some sort.

Specifically, Section A, Part II of Form 2106 is subtitled: *Vehicle Expenses: General Information.* On this portion of the form, there are **seven** line entries which must be completed. ALL must be completed; none can be left blank. This is the "written information" that must be provided to the IRS, before any of your auto expenses become allowable.

In edited/abbreviated form, the seven line entries are:

1. Date vehicle place in service   ____/____/____

2. Total miles driven for the year   _____ mi

3. Business miles included on line 2   _____ mi

4. Percent of business use (Divide line 3 by line 2) _____ %

5. Average daily round trip commuting distance _____ mi

6. Commuting miles included on line 2   _____ mi

7. Other personal miles included on line 2   _____ mi

The key to making these entries properly is to enter your commute miles first. This entry line (line 6 above) is a guaranteed target for cross-checking by the IRS. DO NOT LEAVE THE COMMUTE MILEAGE LINE BLANK!

Commute mileage, if you recall from Chapter 1, is the distance from your personal home to your tax home, and back again. You

BUSINESS USE OF AUTO

should document the round-trip distance by means of a road map, highlighting the route you normally take. Typically, there are 250 work days per year (5 days per week x 50 weeks, with 2 weeks off for vacation). Therefore, your commute mileage should be 250 times your average daily commute distance. If not, be prepared to explain.

When your commute mileage is not 250 times your round-trip commute, it is a good idea to place an asterisk (*) alongside of the commute figure that you do show. Then explain in synoptic form the "deficiency." Your explanation(s) could be—

(a) You don't go to your tax home every day
— you go directly to another job site several times a week
— you are away overnight on business x days a week
(b) Your office is in your personal home
— as per agreement with your employer
— you go to your tax home irregularly
(c) You live quite close to your tax home
— you commute by walking, bicycling, or motorcycling.

Most Expenses Qualify

Once you establish your BUP (business use percentage) for each business-use vehicle, virtually all expenses associated with that vehicle are tax qualified. That is, the total of such expenses times your BUP is tax deductible. The term "all expenses" means all operating and ownership expenses. The only exceptions are fines, penalties, and optional accessories. Otherwise, there is no statutory limit, provided, of course, that you actually incurred the expenses claimed.

What are the vehicle operating/ownership expenses that qualify?

Just about anything and everything that is "ordinary and necessary" for driving the vehicle for business purposes [Sec.162(a)]. This includes gas and oil, repairs, maintenance (lube jobs), tires (and chains), batteries, wiper blades, car washes, driver licenses, registration fees, interest (on car and truck payments), insurance, equipment rentals (such as car phone), and other items (such as auto club dues). Excluded are parking tickets, moving

DEDUCTING JOB EXPENSES

violations, and other vehicular fines. Section 162(f) specifically excludes fines and penalties, to wit:

No deduction shall be allowed under subsection (a) for any fine or similar penalty paid to a government for the violation of any law.

There are certain *allocated* expenses that you can take 100%. No BUP factoring is required. These are parking fees, tolls, garaging fees, towing costs, and accident repairs while on documented business trips. For example, having departed your employment base (tax home), you have an accident en route to a business appointment. The cost of specific repairs and car rental related directly to that business trip are 100% business. If, however, you simultaneously incur other general repairs, such as an engine tune-up, you have to apply the BUP factor.

There is one expenditure category that is a touchy tax issue. It has to do with optional accessories: air conditions, power windows, power seats, cellular phones, computer modems, stereo systems, and the like. The tax issue is: Are these items "ordinary and necessary" for your business driving? Or, are they "luxurious and extravagant" in your case? Count on the IRS to take its usual negative stance that such items are not necessary. If they are truly necessary accessories to accomplish your business tasks, stand your ground. The next issue then will be: Do you expense them or depreciate them? The IRS wants you to depreciate them at least over five years.

Standard Mileage Rate

If keeping detailed account of your actual operating expenses is too much for you, you do have one "safe harbor" recourse. You can elect to use the standard *cents-per-mile* rate. This is an optional method in lieu of actual operating expenses, including depreciation.

So long as you keep track of your business-only miles — this means keeping a true mileage diary — you can use the optional method. In addition, you must own the vehicle yourself, or be buying it under a payment contract. The cost of the vehicle is

BUSINESS USE OF AUTO

irrelevant. The standard rate applies whether the auto is used for local transportation or overnight travel. However, if you elect this optional method, you must do so in the very first year you use your car for business. If you do not use the standard mileage rate in the first year, you may not use it for that car for any subsequent year.

The standard mileage rate is *approximately* 30 cents per mile. We say "approximately" because it changes from year to year (in 1/2- or 1-cent increments). In 1990, for example, it was 26 cents per mile; in 1992 it was 28 cents per mile; in 1996, it was 32 cents per mile. So be sure to check the official IRS instructions before making your final computations. The standard mileage rate applies only to your business-use miles.

For a given vehicle, once the standard mileage rate is elected, it must be used for the entire year. You cannot use the mileage rate for part of the year, and actual expenses for another part of the year. You can, however, use the standard mileage rate for one vehicle, and actual expenses for an entirely separate vehicle in the same year.

For any full taxable year, you can abandon the optional method of prior years and use the actual expense method . . . with straight-line depreciation only. There is just one catch. After 60,000 miles of business use, the vehicle is deemed fully depreciated. Thereafter, you can use either the standard mileage rate or your actual expenses, *without* depreciation.

Limited Cost Recovery

There was a time (prior to 1986) when the concept of depreciation meant that one could recover his capital cost of a business asset over its economically useful life. In the case of a passenger auto, for example, if 100% used in business, its full cost could be recovered in three years. It made no difference what the initial cost was: $10,000; $25,000; $40,000 . . . or higher. One could recover his entire cost (less salvage or trade-in value). This recovery was in the form of an "allowed or allowable" depreciation deduction.

Today, for passenger vehicles, some depreciation recovery is allowed, but not the full cost. The modern (post-1986) rationale is *limited cost recovery*. That is, no matter what the initial cost of one's

DEDUCTING JOB EXPENSES

business-use vehicle may be, the amount of depreciation deduction is very — very — limited. We call this: "limited depreciation shock."

The first shock is that any passenger auto must be depreciated over five years: not three years as formerly. This is so decreed in tax code Section 168(e)(3)(B)(i): *Classification of Certain Property*. Specifically, this subsection says—

> *The term "5-year property" includes—*
> *(i) any automobile or light general purpose truck.*

The second shock is that the amount of depreciation allowable for each of the five years is severely limited. The maximum possible depreciation recovery each year is set forth in Section 280F(a)(1)(A): **Limitation on Amount of Depreciation for Automobiles.** In introductory part, this section reads as—

> *The amount of the depreciation deduction for any taxable year for any passenger automobile shall not exceed—*
> *(i) $2,560 for the 1st taxable year in the recovery period,*
> *(ii) $4,100 for the 2nd taxable year in the recovery period,*
> *(iii) $2,450 for the 3rd taxable year in the recovery period, and*
> *(iv) $1,475 for each succeeding taxable year in the recovery period.*

As per subsection 280F(d)(7), the above recovery amounts are adjusted upward each year for automobile price inflation. The adjustments are in increments of $100, and are based on the Consumer Price Index (CPI) published by the Department of Labor. The base-reference year after which the CPI adjustments apply is 1987. As a rough estimate, one could use a CPI adjustment of between 3% and 5% per year. It is not a significant factor in altering the limitations listed.

Using the base amounts above (unadjusted for CPI), the 5-year depreciation deduction for a vehicle used 100% in business is $12,060 (2,560 + 4,100 + 2,450 + 1,475 + 1,475). With CPI adjustments to 1996, the maximum possible cost recovery is $14,460, regardless of the business-use auto's actual cost!

BUSINESS USE OF AUTO

Each of the above deduction amounts is modified by the BUP of the vehicle for each taxable year. Thus, if the average BUP of your vehicle over the 5-year period is 63%, say, the maximum depreciation deduction (cost recovery) that you can take is $9,110 ($14,460 x 63%). This is shocker No. 3.

Using this 63% BUP example, suppose you bought a $30,000 auto for business use, and installed $7,110 in optional accessories. Your total capital investment would be $37,110. Under the limited cost recovery rationale, at the end of five years you would still have an *unrecovered cost* of $28,000 (37,110 – 9,110).

Wouldn't an unrecovered cost of $28,000 have some dampening effect on the amount of money that you would be willing to put into a business auto? Taxwise, wouldn't you be just as well off buying an "economy auto": one costing less than $15,000?

Luxury Auto Leasing

There is temptation in thinking that there's some magic in leasing a luxury auto (for business) rather than buying and owning one. Leasing is certainly a practical option, and it may even have some net bottom line tax advantage. But it is not magic.

If you lease an auto for business, whether luxury or otherwise, you still have to establish your qualified business use percentage (BUP). There's no way around it. This means that you have to keep a contemporaneous mileage log, with its collateral supporting evidence. On this matter, there is no distinction between leasing and buying. Leasing does not eliminate all recordkeeping.

Not all auto leasing contracts are pure leases. More often than not, they are leases with options to buy. At the end of the lease period you are expected to buy the vehicle or pay a large penalty to the lessor for not doing so. If you do not have a pure lease, your tax treatment is no different from buying the car. So, check your lease carefully on this point. Most car rental companies offer pure leases, where most car sales companies do not. A pure lease is when you can turn the car in at the end of the contract . . . and walk away.

If you do have a pure lease, there is considerable simplicity in your tax accounting. You only have to keep track of your operating expenses (gas, oil, repairs, insurance, etc.) and your lease payments.

DEDUCTING JOB EXPENSES

Furthermore, if you had month-to-month leases, and used two or three different cars for the taxable year, you don't have to distinguish between them. You can combine all the operating expenses and all the lease payments. You can even combine the business miles, so long as you keep track of the total business-plus-nonbusiness miles driven. That BUP again.

With leasing, your tax computation is as simple as 1, 2, 3. The procedure is as follows:

1. Total operating expenses   _____
2. Total lease payments   _____
3. ADD items 1 and 2   _____
4. MULTIPLY item 3 by your BUP ▶ _____

You get no interest deduction nor depreciation deduction. These items are included in your lease payments. Also included is the profit factor to the lessor. You also can include in the lease payments the rental of optional accessories. None of this comes cheap. However, if you use the leased auto predominantly in business (well over 50%), whatever you pay, times your BUP, is — except for one catch — tax deductible.

What's the catch?

As taxpayer-lessee, you are subject to an **inclusion amount**. That is, you have to *subtract* from your lease payments a specified amount (as determined by the IRS) [IRC Sec. 280F(c)(2), (3)].

In tax theory, the "inclusion amount" approximates the Section 280F(a) limitations you would have been subjected to, had you purchased the vehicle instead of leasing it. The objective — as depicted in Figure 7.2 — is to make the two options (buy or lease) comparable — or tax neutral.

Leased Auto "Inclusion Tables"

The IRS has prepared a number of Leased Luxury Auto Tables. The subheading on each table is *Inclusion Amount for Cars With a Lease Term Beginning in Calendar year*_____. The year of the table corresponds with the beginning of your lease term. The table year reflects the latest auto price inflation adjustment and the latest

BUSINESS USE OF AUTO

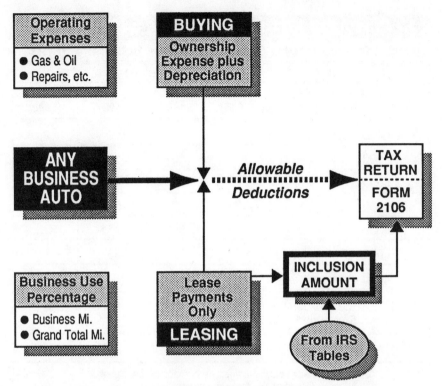

Fig. 7.2 - Buying Versus Leasing of a Business-Use Auto

change in tax law. The tables extend from just under $15,000 in vehicle value to as high as $250,000 in value. Selected portions of Table 5 (for leases beginning in 1994) are presented in Figure 7.3.

The fair market value (FMV) of the leased auto is defined as its value on the first day of the lease term. Therefore, to avoid any FMV dispute with the IRS several years into your lease term, make sure that your contract designates clearly therein the FMV at start of the lease. On this point, Regulation 1.280F-5T(h)(2) says—

If the capitalized cost of listed property is specified in the lease agreement, the lessee shall treat such amount as the fair market value of the property.

Instructions in Regulation 1.280F-7(a)(2) direct that the inclusion amount be determined as follows:

DEDUCTING JOB EXPENSES

Leased Luxury Auto Table 5 [1994]
Inclusion Amounts for Cars With Leases Beginning in 1994

FMV (Fair Market Value)	Tax Year During Lease				
	1st (1994)	2nd (1995)	3rd (1996)	4th (1997)	5th (1998)
$ 14,600 *	0	1	1	2	2
20,000	39	85	127	152	176
30,000	111	244	363	435	503
35,000	146	322	478	573	662
40,000	182	399	593	711	822
50,000	252	555	822	987	1,141
60,000 ▲	327	717	1,065	1,276	1,475

* This is the maximum cost recovery for a buyer-owned vehicle over a 5-yr period (100% BUP).

▲ The official table lists 85 separate FMV values

CAUTION: These selections are for illustration purposes only. Obtain official table for your lease year.

Fig. 7.3 - Selections from IRS Leased Auto Inclusion Table [1994]

1. Corresponding to the FMV, select from the applicable table (and lease term year) the dollar amount prescribed.
2. Prorate the dollar amount for the number of days in the lease term in the taxable year at issue.
3. Include the computed amount (for the year at issue) on Form 2106, page 2, at the line marked: **Vehicle rentals: Inclusion amount.**

The instructions on Form 2106 tell you to subtract the inclusion amount from the total rental payments for the year, BEFORE applying your BUP factor. As illustrated in Figure 7.3, the inclusion amounts are rather modest when compared to the actual value of the vehicle being leased. For example, for a $35,000 vehicle, the total 5-year inclusion amount (before BUP) is about

BUSINESS USE OF AUTO

$2,180 (about $3,760 for a $50,000 vehicle, $5,910 for a $70,000 vehicle).

The only relief from the inclusion requirement is when an auto is rented for less than 30 days. This exception (Sec. 280F(c)(2)) is to accommodate short overnight trips on business and other occasional car rentals.

Employer-Provided Autos

Some companies provide passenger autos to designated employees, where the use of such vehicles can be shown to be directly connected with company business. Where there is predominantly business use of such vehicles (more than 50%), it is operationally more advantageous for the company to provide the vehicles rather than expecting employees to provide their own. When this is done, personal use by the employees is often permitted.

A company-provided vehicle to a designated employee can be treated as 100% business use by the employer (NOT by the employee) . . . IF. There are two "if" conditions. One or the other must prevail. These conditions are:

1. If the value of the personal use by the employee is *included in income* of such employee and subject to withholdings, OR
2. If the value of personal use by the employee results in *payment of rent* to the company, and the company reports it as "other income" subject to tax.

If either of the conditions is met, whether the company buys or leases the vehicles, *each vehicle* is treated separately as 100% used in that company's business. The rationale for 100% business use is that any personal use by employees is income taxed. It is taxed either as income to the employee, or as income to the company. One way or the other, the personal use is taxed.

For income taxing the personal use of company-provided vehicles, special inclusion-value methods have been IRS approved. There are three such methods, namely:

7-17

DEDUCTING JOB EXPENSES

A. Annual lease value method,
B. Cents-per-mile method,
C. Commuting value method.

Method A is commonly used for officers, managers, and marketing personnel driving luxury autos. Method B is often used for run-of-the-mill employees driving economy autos. Method C is for route drivers, repair technicians, equipment installers, etc., where racks, tools, and parts make passenger-carrying uncomfortable.

Any method may be elected by simply using it for a designated vehicle. Once elected, it must be used consistently for the same vehicle over its useful life. There is no requirement that all vehicles owned by the same company adopt the same method.

The personal use of company autos by designated employees is treated as compensation for services performed and is taxed as a "fringe benefit." This is specifically so stated in Regulation 1.61-21(a): *Taxation of fringe benefits*, to wit—

Examples of fringe benefits include: an employer-provided automobile, a flight on an employer-provided aircraft, . . . [etc.]

The moral to all of Regulation 1.61-21 is: "There are just no free company autos any more."

8

BUSINESS USE OF HOME

> Section 280A(c) Sets The Conditions For Deductibility Of Certain Expenses For Business Use Of Your Home. The Area(s) You Designate As "Office" Must Be Used EXCLUSIVELY As Such. It Becomes Your "Principal Place" Of Business . . . For The CONVENIENCE Of Your Employer. You Need A Statement On Company Letterhead To This Effect. After Which, You Establish By Square Footage Measurements The BUP (Business Use Percentage). Deductible Amounts Are The BUP Portions Of Home Insurance, Repairs And Maintenance, Phone And Utilities, Security Services, Etc. Also Allowable Is A Depreciation Deduction For The BUP Portion Of Your Home Structure And Its Appurtenances.

More and more these days, employees are finding it necessary to use one or more portions of their personal home for business purposes. Many factors in a changing world account for this trend. Perhaps foremost is technology. Desktop computers, workstations, modems, fax machines, copy machines, laser printers, videophone conferencing, E-mail, CD-Rom files, and a whole host of other "electronic gadgets" are available in home office sizes with capacity and capability to match that at the employer's regular place of business. Why go to an office on your employer's premises when you can do the same work at home, and still deal with the same bosses, employees, customers, prospects, and vendors?

Other factors in home office attractiveness are commuting congestion, air pollution, and at-work parking. More and more, the

DEDUCTING JOB EXPENSES

infrastructure of traditional business centers is breaking down because too many workers are going to and from at approximately the same time in approximately the same directions. For some business functions, *telecommuting* makes real sense. But the IRS has yet to recognize this as a positive factor in contributing to the greater productivity of this nation.

Still another factor in the home office trend is the downsizing, decentralization, and the national/international networking of businesses on the information superhighway. The day of big business — and big government — with its autocratic headquarters and bureaucratic branch offices is easing from sight. More and more, these centers of control are evolving into electronic dispatching of information and instructions to and from home office employees, mobile field workers, remote site vendors, and in-flight salespersons.

But, before you think too rationally on modern-day trends, you have to watch your Ps and Qs on the tricky tax rules for home office deductions. The IRS just loves to stop you cold with its Section 280A: *Disallowance of Certain Expenses in Connection with Business Use of Home, Etc.* We have to explain this "disallowance mentality" to you in order for you to understand its exceptions. Under certain conditions — Section 280A(c) — you **can** deduct your home office operation expenses.

Self-Motivated, Self-Doers Only

Not every employee can nor should work at home. Only certain types with certain talents should do so. The best candidates are those who are self-motivated and self-doers. They are given a broad job assignment with specific tasks . . . and they're off on their own. These types include outside salespersons, marketing reps, staff consultants, software developers, technical writers, claims processors, purchasing agents, and other independent-minded workers who can work at home in an efficient and productive manner.

The convenience to the employer — and employee — of working at home is unsurpassed. The work scheduling is NOT a fixed 8-hour-day, 5-days-a-week activity. There are times when

BUSINESS USE OF HOME

there are 12-hour days, 6 1/2 days a week. There are also times when there are 4-hour days and 4-day weeks. In certain types of businesses, customers, clients, and vendors like knowing that they can reach designated employees at home during normally off hours. In fact, off-hour access is one of the star competitive advantages that home office workers have over traditional-type, centralized business enterprises. Sometimes, though, this ready access for off-hour business can interfere with personal and family living. This is especially true of a home-working parent with minor children. This is where the home office deduction rules make sense. They require that a regular and exclusive work area be maintained.

There is no question that, if you can conduct the major portion of your employer's business out of your home, you can make it into a very efficient operation. You are not dependent on the whims and vacillations of bosses, co-workers, suppliers, vendors, and government agents. You can organize your work routine, streamline your operation, and simplify your recordkeeping. If you are truly self-disciplined, you can institute a "clean desk" policy whereby everything has its place and is in its place. No more workplace disorder and confusion, as is typically found in "office offices" in centralized business or manufacturing districts.

If you are allowed to work at home for the convenience of your employer, you must set realistic goals of accomplishment. You need to display an inner drive and agenda that moves you on. You set reasonably regular schedules for your business contacts locally, nationally, and internationally. Your home office is where you can be your own boss, yet be associated with an employer whose products or services you are eager to advance.

Introduction to Section 280A(c)

The IRS has always chafed at allowing any deduction against gross income for expenses incurred while working out of one's home. For some reason, this is an area of endeavor that tax agents simply can't comprehend as being a necessity of modern business.

This is a throwback to 1954 when the IRS induced Congress to enact Section 262 of the IR Code. This section, titled: **Personal, Living, and Family Expenses,** says, in its subsection (a) that—

DEDUCTING JOB EXPENSES

Except as otherwise provided . . . , no deduction shall be allowed for personal, living, and family expenses.

This is clear and concise: "no deductions shall be allowed."

With Section 262(a) as its mandate, the IRS has been quite successful at maximizing revenue by arbitrarily disallowing all business-use-of-home expenses.

Finally, in 1986 Congress came to its senses and amended a portion of the law it had enacted in 1975 disallowing expenses in connection with . . . *the use of a dwelling unit* [Sec. 280A]. It amended Section 280A to include a new subsection (c): ***Exceptions for Certain Business or Rental Use.*** This subsection, comprising approximately 900 words, is arranged into six paragraphs, namely:

(1) Certain business use;
(2) Certain storage use;
(3) Rental use;
(4) Providing day care services;
(5) Limitations on deductions;
(6) Treatment of rental to employer.

Paragraph (1) of Section 280A(c) is particularly pertinent to our discussion in this chapter. It reads in full as:

(1) Subsection (a) [relating to "no deduction allowed"] *shall not apply to any item to the extent such item is allocable to a portion of the dwelling unit which is used exclusively on a regular basis—*
(A) as the principal place of business for any trade or business of the taxpayer,
(B) as a place of business which is used by patients, clients, or customers in meeting or dealing with the taxpayer in the normal course of his trade or business, or
(C) in the case of a separate structure which is not attached to the dwelling unit, in connection with the taxpayer's trade or business.

BUSINESS USE OF HOME

In the case of an employee, the preceding sentence shall apply only if the exclusive use referenced to in the preceding sentence is for the convenience of his employer.

Thus, right off, there are one or more of three alternative conditions to be met, in order to circle around the "no deduction allowed" mandate. Any one alternative will satisfy the exception provision; any two alternatives will satisfy; or all three.

Regular and Exclusive Use

There is a basic umbrella requirement to be met for all alternatives (A), (B), and (C). That is, the designated (as business) portion of the dwelling unit must be used . . . *exclusively on a regular basis*. This is the "exclusive use" test which the IRS makes much ado about.

As defined in Regulation 1.280A-2(g), the test for exclusivity is met—

. . . only if there is no use of that portion of the unit at any time during the taxable year other than for business purposes. [Emphasis added.]

This means that there can be no personal, family, or recreational use — at any time — of that portion of your home which you designate for business. Indications of nonbusiness use would be the existence of television, pool table, sofa bed, comfortable lounge, children's toys, storage of wearing apparel, and other accouterments of everyday living. Temporary entry by family members and others for cleaning, maintenance, and repairs does not defeat the exclusivity test.

Regulation 1.280A-2(g) goes on to say that—

*The phrase "a portion of the dwelling unit" refers to a room or other **separately identifiable space**; it is not necessary that the portion be marked off by a permanent partition.* [Furthermore], *the portion . . . may be used for more than one business purpose.* [Emphasis added.]

DEDUCTING JOB EXPENSES

Regulation 1.280A-1(c)(1) defines a "dwelling unit" as—

A house, apartment, condominium, mobile home, boat, or similar property, which provides basic living accommodations such as sleeping space, toilet, and cooking facilities. A single structure may contain more than one dwelling unit. All structures and other property appurtenant to a dwelling unit . . . are considered part of the unit.

What all of this is saying is that, if you designate a separately identifiable portion of your home for business use, and you use it regularly as such, it *may* qualify as business property. If so, the allocable expenses therewith would be deductible.

Principal Place of Business

Once the umbrella test of exclusive use is met, the first statutory alternative is the "principal place" test. This is alternative (A), otherwise designated as Section 280A(c)(1)(A). This rule requires that the designated business-use portion of your home be the principal place for conducting your business. If your home is the only place where you conduct business, there is no interpretation problem. But suppose you have two or more places for doing business, which one is the principal place?

For example, suppose you are an outside sales person (or technical writer, or claims adjuster, or purchasing agent, etc.). Your job description requires that you explore all possible sales leads; that you make all of your own appointments for meeting and dealing with potential and existing customers; and that you visit regularly-in-person your employer's major customers. You are expected to nurture certain customers' every need and whim, even if you have to visit their places of business several times a week (or several times a month). Servicing certain accounts may require that you spend more actual time out of your home office than in it. Where is your principal place of business: at home or on the road?

Is one's principal place of business the "focal point" of his operations or is it the "dominant place" where he spends most of his time? What are the facts and circumstances involved? To "meet

BUSINESS USE OF HOME

and deal" with customers (or suppliers, or vendors, or other employees), must you do so only through their physical presence in your home, or can you do so by means of online computers, videophones, and/or fax machines?

A sensible approach to the principal-place decision is an intelligent weighing of various business factors. Among the factors that the IRS and the Tax Court will consider are the following:

1. The length of time spent at home on business compared with the time spent elsewhere.
2. The importance of the business functions performed at home, compared with those performed elsewhere.
3. The necessity and suitability of an office at home, compared with its incidental availability elsewhere.
4. The availability of adequate office, shop, or storage space, including telephone and business privacy, at locations other than at one's home.
5. The amount of expertise, and the nature of the organizational and management activities, essential to conducting the business, relative to those activities that generate the income.

Many of the IRS assertions of your principal place of business are based on its hasty judgment calls. It is so easy for the IRS to say "No." But, as a dedicated home office employee, you have to be more forceful in standing up to the IRS. Towards this end, the "facts and circumstances" that you should be loaded with are presented in Figure 8.1. The principal place test is the most controversial of the three Section 280A(c) alternatives.

Much To-Do About *Soliman*

So abstract and controversial is the term "principal place," that the matter went to the U.S. Supreme Court for interpretation. After **10 years** of the IRS's litigative hassling of taxpayer *Nader E. Soliman*, the High Court ruled that there can be situations in which there may be no principal place of business, and, therefore, no home office deduction. Eight of the nine justices held to this view; one

DEDUCTING JOB EXPENSES

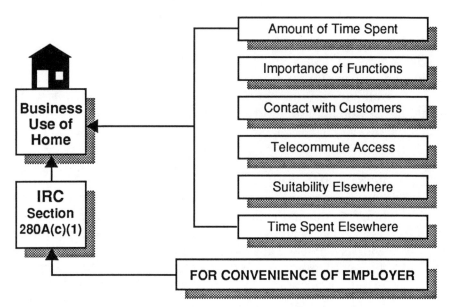

Fig. 8.1 - "Testing Factors" for Employee's Principal Place of Business

justice dissented [*Commissioner IRS v. Soliman*, 93-1 USTC ¶ 50,014].

Taxpayer *Soliman* was an anesthesiologist working at three different hospitals in Maryland and Virginia. At each hospital, he administered the anesthesia, cared for patients after surgery, and treated those with lingering pain. None of the hospitals provided him with an office. So, he set up a separate room in his home and used it exclusively as an office. He spent two or three hours each day there contacting patients, surgeons, and the hospitals by phone; maintaining patient logs and billing records; preparing for treatments and medications; and satisfying his continuing medical education requirements.

On his **1983** return, *Soliman* claimed deduction for the portion of his condominium fees, utilities, insurance, and depreciation attributable to his home office. Upon audit, the IRS disallowed all of these expenses. Upon petition, the Tax Court ruled in favor of *Soliman* and against the IRS. The IRS, in turn, appealed to the Fourth Circuit Court of Appeals in Richmond, Virginia. The Court of Appeals also ruled in *Soliman's* favor.

The Appeals Court held that—

BUSINESS USE OF HOME

Where management or administrative activities are essential to the taxpayer's trade or business, and the only available office space is the taxpayer's home, the "home office" can be his "principal place of business" . . . [where]:

(1) the office in the home is essential to the taxpayer's business;

(2) he spends a substantial amount of time there; and

(3) there is no other location available for performance of the office functions of the business.

Not satisfied with this interpretation, the IRS — using taxpayer money and taxpayer-paid attorneys — appealed the Fourth Circuit's ruling to the U.S. Supreme Court. In an approximately 5,000-word rationale of sophisticated juristic theories, focusing on the word "principal," the High Court majority concluded that *Soliman—*

*Was **not** [Emphasis added] entitled to a deduction for home office expenses. The practice of anesthesiology requires the medical doctor to treat patients under conditions demanding immediate, personal observation . . . at hospitals. The actual treatment was the essence of the professional service. We can assume that careful planning and study were required in advance of performing the treatment, and we acknowledge that this was done in the home office. But . . . the home office activities . . . must be regarded as less important to the business of the taxpayer than the tasks he performed at the hospitals.*

The 10 to 15 hours per week spent in the home office measured against the 30 to 35 hours per week at the three hospitals are insufficient to render the home office the principal place of business. That the office may have been essential is not controlling.

The judgment of the Court of Appeals is reversed.
[January 12, 1993]

It is rulings like this — draining 10 years (1983 to 1993) of *Soliman's* money and time — that incites the IRS to perpetually go

DEDUCTING JOB EXPENSES

against the statutory intent of Congress. None of the concurring justices ever experienced the combat of competition in the real world workplace. From their ivory towers of academia, prestigious law firms, and government appointments, they have life tenure in a taxpayer-paid sanctuary. Why couldn't they use ordinary common sense, as the one dissenting justice did?

The One Sensible Opinion

Although overruled by the High Court majority in the *Soliman* case, Justice Stevens offered the only dissenting opinion. It was sensible in its rationale of the legislative intent of Congress. Among his dissenting comments were:

> *Respondent* [Soliman] *is self-employed. He pays the ordinary and necessary expenses associated with the operation of his office* [in his home]; *it is the only place of business that he maintains. In my opinion, the Tax Court and the Court of Appeals correctly concluded that the respondent is entitled to an income tax deduction for the cost of maintaining that office. This Court's contrary conclusion misreads the term "principal place of business" in* [IRC Sec. 280A(c)], *deviates from Congress' purpose in exacting that provision, and unfairly denies an intended benefit to the growing number of . . . taxpayers who manage their business from a home office.*

Justice Stevens' dissenting opinion went on to point out that the Court's rationale seemed to be based on the premise that: "the taxpayer's house does not become a principal place of business by default." The fact that *Soliman* had no other office was not justification to the majority that he had a place of business. "It is clear," Justice Stevens went on to say, "that Congress intended only to prevent deductions for home offices that were not genuinely necessary business expenses." He further pointed out that IRC Sec. 280A(c)(1) prescribes three **equally-valued** alternatives: (A) **or** (B) **or** (C), and that the Court gave a higher priority to (B) — place for meeting and dealing with patients, clients, or customers — than Congress intended.

BUSINESS USE OF HOME

Justice Stevens concluded his dissent by writing that—

*In my judgment, a principal place of business is a place maintained by or . . . for the business. As I would construe the statute in this context, respondent's office is not just the "principal" place of his trade or business; it is the **only** place of his . . . business.*

Fortunately for us all, Congress actually read Justice Stevens' dissenting opinion. It incorporated the essence of that opinion into an amendment to Section 280A(c)(1)(A). The amendment reads—

For purposes of subparagraph (A), the term "principal place of business" includes a place of business which is used by the taxpayer for the administrative or management activities of any trade or business of the taxpayer if there is no other fixed location of such trade or business where the taxpayer conducts substantial administrative or management activities of such trade or business.

This amendment is effective commencing January 1, 1999.

Get Statement from Employer

The *Soliman* case dealt primarily with self-employed persons. Yet, the "place of business" interpretive issues are identical to those for employees. So if, as an employee, you legitimately work out of your home, do not hesitate to claim your office-at-home expenses. The best way to do this is to get a statement from your employer, on the company letterhead. The thrust of the statement should be that you are allowed/expected/required to work out of your home "for the convenience" of the trade or business indicated by the letterhead. Most employers are timid/reluctant about providing such a statement. Still, you MUST HAVE it.

Where do we get the phrase "for the convenience of" your employer? It is in the very last sentence in Section 280A(c)(1), previously quoted in full. For *your* convenience, we'll requote that sentence in emphasized form:

DEDUCTING JOB EXPENSES

In the case of an employee, the preceding sentence [regarding "certain business use" of a portion of one's home] *shall apply only if the exclusive use referred to in* [that] *sentence is for the convenience of his employer.*

Therefore, in a tactful and persuasive manner, request that your employer provide you with a TO WHOM IT MAY CONCERN letter, with preamble words along the following lines—

Pursuant to the statutory intent of Internal Revenue Code Section 280A(c)(1), last sentence, the use of an office at home by our employee, _____(your name)_____ , is for the express convenience of the trade or business of (your employer's company name).

Then, list separately such convenience-serving factors as:

1. That the nature of your job (describe it, your "territory" and duties) requires independent performance at various hours and at various places.

2. That no office (or no suitable office) is available (or is expected to be made available) on the company's premises on a regular basis.

3. That you are expected to (and/or are required to) procure on your own (with or without assistance from the company) all necessary office equipment and devices for compatible telecommunicating with the company, its customers, vendors, clients, employees, etc. on a regular (or irregular) basis.

4. That the company is decentralizing various employee functions so as to increase its competitiveness and efficiency, and to minimize commuting congestion and air/water pollution.

The sign-off words should be along the lines that, although your work-station "assignment" is at your home (state the address), you are expected to visit company premises from time to time for group meetings, update sessions, and progress reporting.

Try by every means possible to get a statement from your employer along the lines above. We caution you, however, that most employers feel threatened and intimidated by the IRS, and are afraid to put anything in writing that might be misconstrued by that

BUSINESS USE OF HOME

agency. So don't expect much willing cooperation. But, try you must. When successful, label it as **Statement 1**. There will be other "statements" that you will need when preparing for the home-office onslaught. We give you a chronological listing of them in Figure 8.2.

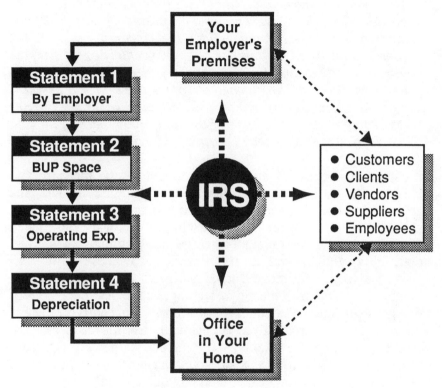

Fig. 8.2 - Statements Needed for Office-in-Home Deduction

Business Use Percentage

Regardless of the type of business activity conducted in or out of your home, the portion allocable to such use must be established with specificity. The designated portion(s) must be identified as some fixed percentage of the total dwelling unit space. For this, *measured square footage* becomes the yardstick for tax

DEDUCTING JOB EXPENSES

accountability. Guessing and off-the-cuff estimates are not acceptable.

Regulation 1.280A-2(i)(3) addresses the business-use-of-home percentage as follows:

> *The taxpayer may determine the expenses allocable to the portion of the* [dwelling] *unit used for business purposes by any method that is reasonable under the circumstances. If the rooms in the dwelling unit are of approximately equal size, the taxpayer may ordinarily allocate the general expenses for the unit according to the number of rooms used for the business purpose. The taxpayer may also allocate general expenses according to the **percentage of the total floor space** in the unit that is used for the business purpose.* [Emphasis added.]

The best specificity approach is to get a tape measure and measure the outside dimensions (length and breadth) of the partitions or walls that separate the business space of use. So long as there is a bona fide regular and exclusive use of the designated space, measure it. This includes garage areas, storage areas, toilet areas, hallway areas, waiting room areas . . . whatever is used as appropriate to your business. But, be realistic.

You must exclude the eating, sleeping, and recreational areas of your home. You can't deduct a portion of your bedroom even if you have a desk there that you occasionally use for business. The same applies to your kitchen. If you occasionally serve your customers coffee, tea, or snacks, you can't write off a portion of your kitchen. The same also applies to your TV and family room, even though you may keep a few toys to entertain your clients' children when doing business with their parent(s) in your home. Use some common sense.

We highly recommend that you prepare a not-to-scale drawing (plan view) of your home. Shade or emphasize the areas that are used for business. Show the dimensions of these areas in feet and inches. Also show the overall dimensions (total area) of your home. Multiply the length and breadth of each area to establish the square footage of that area. If there is more than one floor to your home, measure the area on each floor where there is business use.

BUSINESS USE OF HOME

As an illustration of what we are getting at, we present Figure 8.3. For your own records, you should label such a sketch of your home office as **Statement 2**. Have it available for presentation to the IRS should questions arise. If you do, and it is updated and current, you have a better-than-average chance of your square footages being accepted. We doubt seriously that any IRS agent will go to the effort to measure your home office spaces himself/herself.

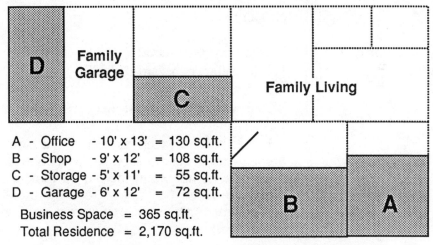

A - Office   - 10' x 13' = 130 sq.ft.
B - Shop   - 9' x 12'   = 108 sq.ft.
C - Storage - 5' x 11'   = 55 sq.ft.
D - Garage   - 6' x 12'   = 72 sq.ft.

Business Space = 365 sq.ft.
Total Residence = 2,170 sq.ft.

Fig. 8.3 - Measurement of Space: Business Use of Home

Using the spaces shown in Figure 8.3, your business use percentage (BUP) would be

$$\text{BUP} = \frac{365 \text{ sq. ft. office space}}{2{,}170 \text{ sq. ft. total residence}} = 0.1682 = 16.82\%$$

If your own BUP should turn out to be less than 5%, we suggest hat you **not** claim the home office deduction. It entails a lot of work for little benefit. On the other hand, if your BUP turns out to be more than 30%, prepare yourself for IRS challenge. The typical acceptable range of BUP is 10% to 25%.

DEDUCTING JOB EXPENSES

List Your Operating Expenses

Once you have established the BUP of your home, you are entitled to deduct certain expenses necessary for operating and maintaining your office *and* your home. Accordingly, the following is a list of the types of expenses that are allowable:

Priority I:
- ☐ real estate taxes
- ☐ acquisition mortgage interest
- ☐ casualty losses

Priority II:
- ☐ equity mortgage interest
- ☐ home insurance (hazard & liability)
- ☐ repairs and maintenance
- ☐ phone and utilities (gas, electricity, water, trash, etc.
- ☐ other expenses [such as rent (if a non-homeowner), security services, pest control, lawn care (if important to your customers), pool service (if used for business entertainment), magazines (if in your waiting room), etc.]

Priority III: ☐ depreciation (of the building structure)

The three priority groupings are because Section 280A(c)(5) — previously listed as "paragraph (5)" — sets a limit on the overall amount of expenses that can be deducted. We won't quote its statutory wording, as it is *very* confusing. Its essence is that the business use of home expenses cannot produce a net loss to you as an employee.

The Priority I expenses are those items that you would be allowed, irrespective of whether your home is used for business or not. These expenses go on Schedule A (1040): Itemized Deductions. Priority II expenses are typically the kind you would not be allowed, if your home were not used for business. Even when used as a business, Priority II expenses are not allowed if your other non-office expenses produced a business loss. These

BUSINESS USE OF HOME

expenses you list on a separate worksheet which you label as **Statement 3**. Priority III, depreciation expense, will depend on the amount of business profit remaining, if any, after the Priority II expenses are deducted. These expenses also go on a separate worksheet which you label as **Statement 4**.

As to your Statement 3 expenses (insurance, repairs, utilities, etc.: Priority II above), the home office instructions suggest that you allocate those expenses into two columnar groupings: (a) Direct expenses, and (b) Indirect expenses. The instructions tell you that the distinction between column (a) and column (b) is that:

Direct expenses benefit only the business part of your home. They include painting or repairs made to the specific area or room used for business. Enter 100% of your direct expenses on the appropriate line in column (a).

Indirect expenses are for keeping up and running your entire home. They benefit both the business and personal parts of your home. Generally, enter 100% of your indirect expenses on the appropriate expense line in column (b).

Upon totaling all entries in each column, the column (a) items are 100% business. The column (b) items are your BUP% business. That is, you multiply the column (b) total by your BUP then add such amount to the column (a) total. The worksheet arrangement for doing so is presented in Figure 8.4. This is the kind of format that your Statement 3 should look like as a backup to each home office expense entry on your tax return.

Depreciation of Home Structure

When one claims legitimately on office-in home, he is entitled to a certain amount of depreciation allowance on the building structure of that home. This provides some additional tax write-off against employment income. Of itself, the allowable home office depreciation is not spectacular. But as the saying goes: every little bit helps.

DEDUCTING JOB EXPENSES

Itemized Operating Expenses: Office-in-Home				
ITEM	Col. (a) Direct	Col. (b) Indirect	
Equity Mortgage Interest			
Insurance on Home			• Office Space ___ sq.ft.
• Hazard			
• Liability			
Repairs & Maintenance			
• Cleaning			
• Painting			• Total Area of Home ___ sq.ft.
• Plumbing			
• Electrical			
• Other (list)			
Phone & Utilities			
• Telephone			BUP=___%
• Electricity			
• Heat & gas			
• Water & trash			
• Garbage			
• Other (list)			
Other Expenses (list)			
• Gardening/pest control			
• Security services			
• Beeper services			
• Cellular phone			
• Online services			
• Other (list)			
TOTALS			
BUP x Col.(b)			
GRAND TOTAL: Add Col. (a) & BUP Col. (b) ▶			
Identify as "Statement 3"			

Fig. 8.4 - Allocation of Office-in-Home Operating Expenses

Depreciation is a tax allowance for the wear and tear and general deterioration of property used in business. This is an established tax

8-18

BUSINESS USE OF HOME

principle of longstanding. But, as an ordinary employee, you may not be familiar with the everyday depreciation-in-business principles. Furthermore, home office treatment involves three fine points that are not well known. Consequently, we want to familiarize you with the basic law, so that you'll feel more comfortable claiming depreciation should it be of tax value to you.

The basic depreciation law is Section 167(a). It reads in full as—

There shall be allowed as a depreciation deduction a reasonable allowance for the exhaustion, wear and tear (including a reasonable allowance for obsolescence)—
  (1) of property used in a trade or business, or
  (2) of property held for the production of income.

Section 167(b) directs your attention to Section 168: ***Accelerated Cost Recovery System*** (ACRS: a new acronym for depreciation allowance). The only portions of Section 168 that are relevant here are subsections 168(b)(3) and (c)(1). In these subsections you are told to use straight line depreciation over 27.5 years for residential *rental* property, and 39 years for *nonresidential* real property. Now, we pose this question to you: What recovery period do you use for home office depreciation? The tax code is silent on this point. Since a home office is not "residential" (you cannot use it for personal or family living) and it is not being "rented" (by you to someone else), what cost recovery period do you use?

Answer: Use 30 years and don't fret over it. Chances are, you'll never home office it for 30 years anyhow. This is fine point #1.

Another fine point relates to identifying the cost or value of the building *structure*, separately from any land or air to which the structure relates. Taxwise, land and air do not depreciate. Only the building structure — and its appurtenances — depreciate. How do you determine this cost or value?

One way is to use data provided to you by, or requested by you from, your County Assessor's Office. Local assessors usually assess the land and buildings (called "improvements") separately for property tax purposes. Or you can engage a professional appraiser.

DEDUCTING JOB EXPENSES

By whatever means is reasonable, you must establish the cost or value of the structure and appurtenances which house your office, up to the date when it is first used for business purposes. This is *your* responsibility: fine point #2.

Your next step is to apply your home office BUP to the cost or value of the structure. Which do you use: cost **or** value. The term "cost" is your acquisition cost plus all structural improvements and appurtenances up to the date of conversion to business use. The term "value" is what the structure would sell for if it were offered for sale to the general public. The general instructions for office-in-home depreciation tell you to use the **lower** of cost or value. This is fine point #3.

All information pertaining to your depreciation deductions should be summarized in a schedule or statement which we previously suggested being labeled as **Statement 4** (recall Figure 8.2). Later, in Chapter 11, we'll revisit this discussion and present the methodology and format in a numerical example. In the meantime, be informed that, typically, home office depreciation deductions range between $500 and $2,000 per year. Exact amounts, of course, depend on the extent of your BUP and the cost or value of your home.

9

REIMBURSEMENT & RECORDS

> Confusion Arises From Misconceptions Over Reimbursement Accounting. If You Meet "Accountable Plan" And "Deemed Substantiated" Rules, Expense Reimbursements Are "Silent" On Your Return. Otherwise, You Are Subject To FULL ACCOUNTING To The IRS On ALL Claimed Job Expenses. This Means Collecting, Annotating, And Categorizing Receipts, Diaries, And Documents Throughout The Year. Section 274(d) Requires Identifying Such "Elements" As Amount, Date, Place, Description, Business Purpose, And Business Connection. ADEQUATE RECORDS Are Those Which Are Prepared "At Or Near" The Time Of Expenditure Or Use.

To one extent or another, most employees are reimbursed for at least some of the job-related business expenses that they incur. The arrangement for doing so depends on the reimbursement policy(ies) of the employer, the size and activity of the employer, various department "expense budget" caps, and the overall value of the employee in the hierarchy of generating new business and maintaining customer goodwill for the company. Often, the extent of reimbursement is a negotiated affair between the employer and employee. When so "negotiated," the reimbursement policies are seldom set forth in writing.

Nevertheless, the amounts reimbursed — to whatever dollar extent that might be — have to be tax accounted for. Many employees are genuinely confused about this. They consider all

DEDUCTING JOB EXPENSES

expense reimbursement money as nontaxable. They become careless in keeping track of it. As a result, they often wind up paying income tax and social security/medicare tax on their expense money. We tried to forewarn you about this back in Chapter 2: Scrutinizing Form W-2.

The IRS has it both ways. As we said in Chapter 2, it forces employers to include everything interpretable as compensation into Box 1 of Form W-2. Simultaneously, it arbitrarily disallows the unreimbursed expenses that an employee may claim — legitimately — on his return. Despite what the tax laws say, the IRS does not take kindly to employees who claim job-related expenses. It takes a "show me" attitude, whether the expenses are reimbursed or not reimbursed.

Furthermore, if the contractual relationship with your employer implies a right to reimbursement, you must seek that reimbursement before claiming any expenses on your return. If you do not seek any reimbursement at all, the tax presumption is that the expenses you incurred are not "ordinary and necessary" to your present occupation nor to your present employer's trade or business. Thus, in this chapter, we try to clear up some of the confusion between expense accounting to your employer and expense claiming on your tax return. There are just no tax-free expense accounts anymore.

Reimbursement Variations

There is no federal tax law or regulation that mandates a particular reimbursement policy by your employer. Reimbursement practices vary widely between different businesses and different employers: small and large.

Small companies, just starting in business, rarely have any formal policy positions. They "play it by ear," day to day. Maybe they reimburse and maybe they won't. It is sometimes a matter of whim, but mostly a matter of profit protection. Keeping expenses down is one way to enhance the profits of a burgeoning company.

Major corporate goliaths, on the other hand, have stringent, detailed reimbursement policies that are a bureaucracy of their own. Employees must toe the policy line, or their expense claims will be

REIMBURSEMENT & RECORDS

summarily rejected. Many claimants tread in fear of losing their jobs with these corporate goliaths. They do not submit expense reports and reimbursement claims, even when they are entitled to do so. They absorb the cost without reimbursement.

Hence, the gamut of reimbursements can range from zero to 100%. Within this range, the variations are as follows:

1. No Reimbursement
2. Travel Advances
3. Transportation Tickets
4. Partial Reimbursement
5. Contingent Reimbursement
6. Specific Entertainment
7. Union Negotiated Terms
8. Per Diem Allowances
9. Mileage Allowances
10. Monthly Car Allowance
11. Monthly Expense Allowance
12. Full Reimbursement

More often than not, reimbursement policy is a matter of hearsay and trial and error. When policy is in writing, it is often out of date. Or, in large companies, the policy is found in scattered memoranda and operations orders. In those reimbursement cases where expense reports are submitted, the employer requires that all applicable receipts and documents be attached.

Keep Separate Records

It is surprising how many employees do not keep track of the amount of reimbursements paid to them throughout the year. They submit their expense report, voucher, or request on whatever form or in whatever manner that works. They then receive their expense check (or cash) . . . and spend it. They throw away their payment stubs, thinking: "The whole matter is taken care of."

When asked what total reimbursement they received for the year, they are puzzled and upset. They respond typically: "Why do you ask that? It's not taxable money. It's my expense reimbursement. Why does it matter?"

DEDUCTING JOB EXPENSES

We'll tell you why it matters, below. In the meantime, we offer three precautionary suggestions.

Suggestion 1. Every time you submit an expense report, voucher or request to your employer (or customer), retain a coy of it for yourself. Arrange the copies chronologically throughout the year. Do this whether you are reimbursed in full, in part, or not at all.

Suggestion 2. Every time you receive an advance, a reimbursement amount, or a periodic allowance, separately record the event. Do this on a separate ledger of your own, showing date(s) received, amount(s), and type of payment(s). If appropriate, photocopy the reimbursement statement or check and keep with your records.

Suggestion 3. At the end of each tax year, obtain from your employer (or customer) a statement (on his letterhead) of the total amount of expense reimbursement paid to you. You want to verify the payer's total with your own. It does happen, occasionally, that discrepancies — and "computer errors" — will arise to tax haunt you for many years.

Under tax rules now in effect, employers have to report to the IRS the total amount of expense reimbursements paid to you. They are supposed to tell you how much they report. They also are supposed to itemize the specific expense categories for which they reimbursed you. Often, they do not do what they are supposed to do. They rely on their computer printouts and leave it up to you to fish out the information for yourself. The bottom line is that the total reimbursement amount is surreptitiously reported (to the IRS) either on your regular Form W-2 or on a separate Form W-2.

Expense Accounting to Employer

There is one particular exception to your employer's reporting of all amounts reimbursed on Form W-2. This exception applies when there is *adequate accounting* to your employer. The exception

REIMBURSEMENT & RECORDS

is tax characterized as "reimbursements equal to expenses." This exception is also called an "accountable plan" of reimbursement. The procedure is very limited and very strict.

Adequate accounting for "accountable plans" applies only where—

1. The expenses are paid or incurred by the employee solely for the benefit of his employer.
2. The employee is required to and does make a detailed accounting to his employer for the expenses.
3. The employee is paid for the expenses through advances, allowances, reimbursements, or otherwise, or he charges them to the employer directly or indirectly (as through credit cards).
4. The total amount of advancements, reimbursements, and charges does not exceed the expenses.
5. The expenses are related to travel, transportation, lodging, meals, entertainment, gifts, or with respect to the purchase of listed (depreciable) property.
6. The accounting is settled within 60 days after the expenses are paid or incurred.

The requirement for "adequate accounting" has a special meaning. It means that you submit to your employer an account book, diary, log, statement of expense, trip sheet, or similar record with backup documentation. The record must contain information as to each element of travel, entertainment, or gift expenditure, or of an expenditure or use with respect to listed property. The information must be recorded at or near the time of the expenditure or use. All amounts received by the employee during the year (advances, allowances, reimbursements, direct charges, and credit card charges) must be precisely accounted for to your employer.

Adequate accounting means that there must be an exact match of expenses with reimbursements. There must be no excess expense which is not reimbursed. There must be no excess reimbursement over the expenses. In other words, the whole affair becomes a *tax wash*.

For the adequate accounting (tax wash) rule to apply, your employer must take on the role of the IRS. That is, your employer

DEDUCTING JOB EXPENSES

must act in an adversarial capacity. He must exercise control over the amounts paid and must assure that the expenses are truly "ordinary and necessary." To assure this, your expense reports must be subject to audit, verification, and substantiation as though the IRS itself were present. The expense report must be approved by a responsible person who is not the one incurring the expense.

When there is an exact tax wash, your employer is relieved from reporting on Form W-2 the amount if his reimbursement to you. Conversely, you are disenfranchised from claiming on your return any of those submitted expenses which your employer "adjusted " or disallowed. So important is this concept that we portray it in Figure 9.1. The Figure 9.1 depiction applies only to those situations where you are contractually *required* to account to your employer.

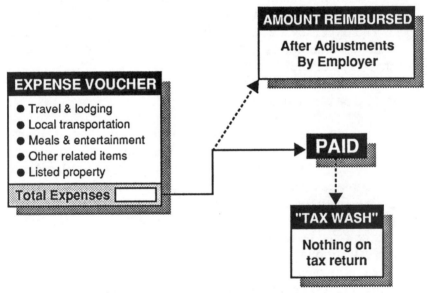

Fig. 9.1 - "Tax Wash" with Expense Accounting to Employer

The Regulatory Language

The adequate accounting to employer (tax wash) rule is a source of much confusion. The confusion arises from the implication that, if one reports any job-related expenses to his employer, and he is reimbursed in whole or part for those expenses, no further tax

REIMBURSEMENT & RECORDS

accounting is needed. This leaves only unreimbursed expenses for recordkeeping and substantiation. This is a misconception.

To help clarify the matter, we should first quote the pertinent portion of the applicable regulation. This would be Regulation 1.162-17(b). The official subheading is: *Expenses for which the employee is required to account to his employer*—

(1) Reimbursements equal to expenses.
(2) Reimbursements in excess of expenses.
(3) Expenses in excess of reimbursements.
(4) Meaning of "to account to"

The subregulation 1.162-17(b)(1) reads, in most part, as—

*The employee need not report on his tax return (either itemized or in total amount) expenses for travel, transportation, entertainment, and similar purposes paid or incurred by him solely for the benefit of his employer for which he is **required to account** and does account to his employer and which are charged directly or indirectly to the employer (for example, through credit cards) or for which the employee is paid through advances, reimbursements, or otherwise, provided the total amount of such advances, reimbursements and charges is equal to such expenses.* [Emphasis added.]

The subregulation 1.162-17(b)(4) also reads in most part as—

*To "account" to his employer . . . means to submit an expense account or other required written statement . . . showing the business nature and the amount of all the employee's expenses . . . **broken down into such broad categories as** transportation, meals and lodging while away from home overnight, entertainment expenses, and other business expenses.* [Emphasis added.]

Filtering through this regulatory language, the key to no tax reporting rests on three points. These points are:

DEDUCTING JOB EXPENSES

One. The employee must be *required* to report all job-related expenses to his employer. If one expense reports to his employer when not required to, his voluntary action does not relieve him of the burden of full reporting on his tax return.

Two. The employee must indeed make the report, and furnish all backup documentation. A handshake and nod of the head will not do. A complete *written report* must be submitted.

Three. The reimbursements must equal the expenses and, conversely, the expenses must equal the reimbursements.

In all other situations, full tax reporting is required. This is required for reimbursed expenses as well as for unreimbursed expenses. Reimbursements in excess of expenses must be employer-reported as income in Box 1 of Form W-2. Expenses in excess of reimbursements may be claimed as deductions on the employee's return. Unreimbursed expenses may be tax claimed, but only after the reimbursed expenses have been accounted for. In other words, if there is so much as $1 "out of match" (pursuant to Figure 9.1), EVERYTHING has to be reported and claimed on your tax return.

Federal Per Diem Allowance

There is some partial relief from reporting/claiming everything on your return. The relief applies to those situations where you agree with your employer to accept Federal per diem rates for lodging, meals, and incidental expenses when traveling away from home on business. Agreeing to accept IRS-published standard allowances is tax treated as *deemed substantiation* of your travel expenses. The only substantiation required is confirmation of the date, place, and business purpose of your travel. This is readily accomplished with lodging receipts only. Excruciating accounting with other receipts is not required. This can save much paperwork both for yourself and your employer. The per diem

REIMBURSEMENT & RECORDS

reimbursements are not included as income on your W-2, nor can you show the amounts as an expense deduction on your return.

There are two categories of Federal per diem rates: domestic and foreign. The domestic rates range from a low of $80 per day (Modesto, California) to a high of $180 per day (New York City). Foreign rates range from a low of $50 (Trinidad, Bolivia) to $370 (Tokyo, Japan). The place of one's overnight lodging constitutes the "travel locality" for selecting the applicable Federal rates.

The per diem rates are published and updated annually by the IRS in tables identified as *Government Travel Allowance Rates*: CONUS (Continental U.S.) and OCONUS (Outside U.S.). The rates include lodging, meals, and incidental expenses (laundry, cleaning, tips, etc.) The per diems do **not** include air fares and local transportation in any form.

In those cases where the employers pay for travel lodging direct, or otherwise provide for it, the IRS tables list M & IE rates (Meals and Incidental Expenses) separately. These M & IE rates may be prorated in 6-hour "quarter days" (midnight to 6 a.m.; 6 a.m. to noon; noon to 6 p.m.; and 6 p.m. to midnight).

The Federal per diem allowances offer a safety net to those employees who travel a lot, and who just hate to keep detailed records of their travel expenditures. Thus, the per diem method can save recordkeeping time and permit the traveler to devote more of his time and effort to business. However, there **is** a downside to this form of "deemed substantiation." Certain employees may find that the standard per diem rates are less than their actual expenses. In addition, the per diems may not be used to substantiate the deduction of unreimbursed expenses.

Prepare for "Full Substantiation"

There is one common purpose behind the rules on adequate accounting to your employer (called: "accountable plans" for reimbursement) and "deemed substantiated." The purpose is to induce taxpayers NOT TO CLAIM travel and other job-necessitated expenditures on their tax returns. When tax returns are silent on job expenses, there are less headaches all around. There are less

DEDUCTING JOB EXPENSES

headaches to your employer, less headaches to you, and — yes — even less headaches to the IRS.

But try to claim $1 in excess of the "silent amounts," and the full wrath of the IRS comes down upon you. At this point, you are confronted with Section 274(d): **Substantiation Required.** This section catapults from Sections 162 and 212 , the two pillars of legitimacy for job expense deductions (recall Figure 1.4), and decrees that—

> *No deduction or credit shall be allowed . . . unless . . .*
> [Emphasis added.]

It is the "unless" part that requires full substantiation by you, if you want to claim your expense deductions on your tax return. Unless you are truly lazy (if you were, you wouldn't be reading this book), and truly hate keeping any kind of expense records at all, we suggest that you hunker down and prepare to substantiate EVERYTHING: *reimbursed* **and** *unreimbursed* alike. For this hunkering down, you need to know more about the specifics of Section 274(d).

On matters of recordkeeping, the essence of Section 274(d) is that each employee claimant must provide the following information:

A. The *amount* of each expense or other item;
B. The *time and place* of the travel or entertainment, the *amount of use* of a facility or property item, and the *date and description* of each gift.
C. The *business purpose* of the expense or other item; and
D. The *business relationship* to the taxpayer of the person(s) entertained, using the facility or property, or receiving a gift.

The manner of satisfying Section 274(d) depends on several factors. It depends on the occupation of the claimant, the nature of his trade or business, the "ordinary and necessary" income-producing aspects, and on the opportunity to prepare contemporaneous records during, or following, the course of one's expensing activities. There is no cast-in-concrete prescribed official

REIMBURSEMENT & RECORDS

recordkeeping form for doing so. Any of the usual forms of daily diaries, ordinary receipts, records of expenditures, and collateral evidence will suffice. No single record is all-purpose serving; no document is self-explanatory entirely on its own.

"Adequate Records" Defined

Section 274(d), referenced above, uses the statutory phrases *adequate records* and *sufficient evidence*. What Congress intended was that the records and evidence be "adequate" and "sufficient" to justify whatever job expense deduction is claimed. These terms are qualitative measures rather than quantitative. As such, they are subject to a wide range of taxpayer and IRS opinions. What may be adequate and sufficient for one trade or business may be wholly inadequate and insufficient for another. The substantiation test, therefore, rests on that which is appropriate and suitable to each separate business activity.

Regulation 1.274-5T(c)(2) is helpful by explaining the adequacy and appropriateness concept. Accordingly, selected portions of this regulation read as follows—

> *To meet the "adequate records" requirements of section 274(d), a taxpayer* **shall maintain** *an account book, diary, log, statement of expense, trip sheets, or similar record . . ., and documentary evidence . . . which,* **in combination**, *are sufficient to establish each element of an expenditure or use. An account book* [etc.] *must be prepared or maintained in such manner that each recording . . . is made* **at or near** *the time of expenditure or use.* [Emphasis added.]

What this regulation is saying is that *written evidence* has considerably more probative value than oral testimony alone. In addition, the probative value of written evidence is greater the closer in time it relates to the expenditure or use. Timely written records — at least on a weekly basis — have a high degree of credibility not present with subsequent statements prepared when generally there is lack of accurate recall.

DEDUCTING JOB EXPENSES

Under some circumstances, it is possible to substantiate an expenditure by other means than timely prepared records. Subregulations 1.274-5T(c)(3) and (4) permit the submission of "other evidence," such as—

   (i) Whether written or oral, containing **specific information in detail** as to such element;
   (ii) By **other corroborative evidence** sufficient to establish such element; [or]
   (iii) Collateral evidence . . . which possesses the **highest degree of probative value** under the circumstances;
such other evidence **shall be considered** to satisfy the substantiation requirements of section 274(d). [Emphasis added.]

Thus, by regulation, it is possible to prove an expenditure by other means than timely prepared records. But don't count on using these alternative proofs for every expense entry on your tax return. You are expected to keep good records as you go along. The alternative proofs are for those situations where the inherent nature of events prevents you from making otherwise timely recordings.

Annotating and Cataloging

The problem with many employee claimants is that they procrastinate. If someone else doesn't prepare a record or document for them, they keep putting off doing it themselves. This is pure inattention and lack of self-discipline. What the regulations are trying to tell you is that if you want a tax deduction, you've got to do your homework. You have to do it consistently and regularly throughout the year.

A particular need for doing so, for example, arises during foreign travel. Most foreign travel is evidenced by documents in the language and currency of the host country. Therefore, immediately after receiving any foreign document, you should handwrite thereon the pertinent English translation and the U.S. dollar equivalents. In most cases, you can get the translation on the spot from those foreign persons who provide the document to you.

REIMBURSEMENT & RECORDS

If you submit a document to an IRS auditor in a foreign language and currency, what do you suppose will happen? Simple: it will be automatically disallowed. Otherwise, how does the IRS know that the document you present is not a foreign vacation or a visit to some ancestral relative?

Similarly, for any other expense document you receive. Make handwritten notes on it: names, items, how related to business, etc. Also, develop a coding system for yourself, for cataloging your documents as you go along. Group them into broad categories such that, when totaled, they fit directly into the proper entry lines on your tax return. For categorization of your job expenses, we suggest the following groupings:

1. Car and truck expenses
2. Other local transportation
3. Travel and lodging away
4. Meals and entertainment
5. Other business expenses
6. Listed property depreciation

There's a knack to categorizing and subcategorizing your job-necessitated expenses. You start by preparing six separate envelopes or folders, as enumerated above. You then set up an "expense chart" of subcategories for each of the six catalog groupings. Tailor each chart to the peculiarities of your own trade or business. Figure 9.2 is intended to provide some thought stimulus in this regard. The whole idea is that you develop into a mechanical collection and collating system that is automatically ready for preparing your tax return at the end of the year.

Separate Reimbursement File

The idea behind Figure 9.2 is that you are preparing yourself for FULL ACCOUNTING on your tax return. You are preparing to do this irrespective of whether your employer reimburses you for some of those expenses or not. On those items for which your employer does reimburse you, prepare a *duplicate* set of documents. Always keep a complete set of records for yourself. When called to the

DEDUCTING JOB EXPENSES

"EXPENSE CHARTING"
CATEGORIES FOR ORGANIZING BUSINESS EXPENSES

Category 1 — Car & Truck Expenses
For vehicles driven by claimant, owned or leased
- Tires, etc.
- Insurance
- Gas & oil
- Repairs
- Car rentals
- Parking & tolls
- Car washes
- Lease payments

Category 2 — Other Local Transportation
Paid to others for doing the driving
- Taxi
- Bus
- Streetcar
- Ridesharing
- Limosine
- Boat
- Train
- Helicopter

Category 3 — Travel & Lodging Away
For sustaining claimant in transit and overnight
- Air tickets
- Intransit snacks
- Sundries & supplies
- Papers & passports
- Lodging
- Baggage handling
- Laundry & cleaning
- Telephone

Category 4 — Meals & Entertainment
Of business guests whether away or not
- Meals (loner)
- Banquets
- Sky boxes
- Beverages
- Sporting events
- Theater
- Meals (w/guests)
- Hunting & fishig

Category 5 — Other Business Expenses
Other than above, yet directly related
- Small gifts
- Small tools
- Dues & publications
- Exhibit fees
- Office-in-home
- Phone & fax
- Repairs & maintenance
- Misc. supplies

Category 6 — Listed Property Depreciation
Items used more than one year, costing over $100
- Autos
- Light trucks
- Computers
- Software
- Cellulars
- Equipment
- Boats
- Aircraft

Fig. 9.2 - Cataloging Job Expenses for Recordkeeping and Backup

substantiation task, the IRS just won't accept the excuse that your employer has part of your records.

REIMBURSEMENT & RECORDS

With the above comment in mind, there is one other — totally separate — recordkeeping task to pursue. Set up an envelope or folder collection system for REIMBURSEMENTS ONLY. This would be a 7th category to the six categories listed in Figure 9.2. But there would be a difference. There would need to be *two* subcategories. We'll call them Column A reimbursements and Column B reimbursements. The terms "Column A" and "Column B" come from Form 2106: *Employee Business Expenses*, which we'll discuss more fully in the next chapter. The Column A reimbursements cover all expenses reimbursed OTHER THAN meals and entertainment. The Column B reimbursement covers meals and entertainment (M & E) only. This two-columnization of reimbursements on Form 2106 is depicted in oversimplified style in Figure 9.3. We just want to impart to you the importance of separating your reimbursements into two classes: non-M & E and M & E.

Form 2106	EMPLOYEE BUSINESS EXPENSES	p.1
	Column A OTHER THAN M&E	**Column B** M&E ONLY
Expense Categories in Fig. 9.2		
X Total Expenses		
Y Amounts Reimbursed		
SUBTRACT Y		
Z Net Expenses		
Deductible (after other adjustments) on Schedule A (1040)		

Fig. 9.3 - The Separation of Employer Reimbursements on Form 2106

The reason for columnar separation of M & E reimbursements is that more substantive supporting and justification elements are

9-15

DEDUCTING JOB EXPENSES

required than expenditure receipts alone. The M & E substantiating elements are covered excruciatingly in Regulation 1.274-5T(b)(3) and (4). This is a particular area where tax auditors go off on their own in probing into your business versus personal motives.

Since every human has to eat and be entertained in some manner, the IRS wants to be sure that, for business deduction purposes, a ***substantial and bona fide*** business discussion has taken place. To attain this assuredness, you can be asked:

1. Did you maintain an M & E diary?
2. If "Yes," is each M & E event logged separately?
3. What was the purpose of each M & E event?
4. Did a substantial business discussion take place: ☐ Before, ☐ During, or ☐ After, the event?
5. Were M & E events held frequently with co-workers?
6. Were M & E events held on the premises of your employer?
7. Was M & E included in a "one price" ticket to all?
8. Did you attend a "qualified" business convention, seminar, or banquet?

After weathering this barrage of M & E questioning, you are then expected to *subtract* the total M & E reimbursements made to you by your employer. Hence, your reimbursements have to be two-columnar as depicted in Figure 9.3. It should be obvious that, unless you take separative steps as you go along throughout the year, a holy mess awaits you at the end of the year.

10

MASTERING FORM 2106

> You Cannot Total Job-Related Expenses And Subtract Them Directly From Gross Income. You Must First Master Your Way Through Form 2106 By Subtotaling Into (1) Vehicle Expenses, (2) Local Transportation, (3) Travel & Lodging, (4) General Business Expenses, And (5) Meals & Entertainment (M & E). After "Allocating" Employer Reimbursements, Residual M & E Is Further Reduced By 50%. Prepare A SEPARATE Form For Each Working Spouse: (H) & (W). The Bottom Line Amount On Each Form 2106 Is Transferred To Schedule A (Form 1040), To Be Further "Whittled Down" Before Deducting From Gross Income.

One of your unwritten job qualifications for employment — which no employer insists that you meet — is knowledge and expertise in the purpose and preparation of Form 2106. If you incur *any* job-related business expenses at all, Form 2106 should be mastered. Like the palm and back of your hand, you should know this form and use it when applicable. Knowing it can save you tax money; not knowing it can cost you tax money. The reality of its importance is that simple.

At various times in previous chapters, we've made reference to Form 2106. We've told you its title before, but we'll cite it again. Its title consists of just three words, namely: *Employee Business Expenses*. Below this official title, there is a small-print instruction which says:

- *Attach to Form 1040*

DEDUCTING JOB EXPENSES

In other words, Form 2106 is an attachment to your regular annual income tax return. This means that you and your working spouse (if any) can complete Form 2106 independently of everything else on your return, then transfer the bottom line results to the designated schedule and line number on your Form 1040.

Among the approximately 5,000 words of official instructions, you are told that—

*Employees who use the standard mileage rate (if claiming vehicle expenses) and are **not** reimbursed by their employers for any expense may file Form 2106-EZ:* **Unreimbursed** *Employee Business Expenses.* [Emphasis added.]

The letters "EZ" mean . . . *Easy.* Sounds like a snap, doesn't it?

Any time a tax form is labeled "EZ," you generally wind up paying higher tax than the corresponding form without these letters. Consequently, we'll not address Form 2106-EZ here. If you master Form 2106 as we think you should, you'll be able to use the EZ version, should it be advantageous to you. Our goal in this chapter is to so familiarize you with Form 2106 that you will look forward eagerly to using it each year. You look forward with the confidence of knowing that you have adequate backup records.

Purpose of Form 2106

The official instructions to Form 2106 say, succinctly—

Use Form 2106 if you are an employee deducting expenses attributable to your job. See the chart [below] *to find out if you must file this form.*

The referenced chart in the instruction is headed: ***Who Must File Form 2106***. The chart is a series of "Yes-No" questions which require you to continue down each "Yes" answer, until the very end. At the end of the 7th "Yes" you are told: *File Form 2106*. If at any time you answer "No," you are told: *Do not file Form 2106*.

MASTERING FORM 2106

The seven questions (abbreviated) are:

1. *Were you an employee during the year?* ☐ *Yes* ☐ *No*
2. *Did you have job-related business expenses?* ☐ *Yes* ☐ *No*
3. *Were you reimbursed for any of your business expenses?* ☐ *Yes* ☐ *No*
4. *Are your deductible expenses more than your reimbursements?* ☐ *Yes* ☐ *No*
5. *Are you claiming job-related vehicle, travel, transportation, meals, or entertainment expenses?* ☐ *Yes* ☐ *No*
6. *Did you use a vehicle in your job?* ☐ *Yes* ☐ *No*
7. *Did you use the actual expense method in the first year you used your vehicle for business?* ☐ *Yes* ☐ *No*

There is also an 8th question directed only at performing artists and disabled employees. For these persons, special rules apply.

An instructional footnote to the official chart of "Yes-No" questions warns that—

Generally, employee expenses are deductible only if you itemize your deductions on Schedule A (Form 1040). Do not file Form 2106 if none of your expenses are deductible because of the 2% AGI limit on Schedule A (Form 1040).

All employees (except performing artists and disabled persons) have to have an aggregate total of business expenses that exceed 2% of their AGI (adjusted gross income) before any Form 2106 expenses are net deductible.

In a nutshell, if your total job expenses are less than $1,000, chances are you'll get no net deduction even if you conscientiously and tediously complete Form 2106. On the other hand, if your total expenses exceed $2,000 (generally), you'd be well advised to use Form 2106 in its entirety. The 2% AGI threshold is speciously known as the "teaser test" prelude to Form 2106.

DEDUCTING JOB EXPENSES

Start on Page 2: Vehicle Expenses

Form 2106 consists of two full pages, front and back. Page 1 is labeled Part I: Employee Business Expenses and Reimbursements. Page 2 is labeled Part II: Vehicle Expenses. The very first data entry line on page 1 is—

Vehicle expenses from [Part II]

The obvious intention is that one must start on page 2/Part II before completing any other line entries on Form 2106. This is because, in most cases, employees use a vehicle (passenger auto or light van) in business to one extent or another.

Page 2/Part II is arranged into four sections, namely:

A — General Information
B — Standard Mileage Rate
C — Actual Expenses
D — Depreciation of Vehicles

An official sidenote to Sections B and D say—

Use this section only if you own the vehicle.

In other words, use of the standard mileage rate or the depreciation deduction (as an allowable expense item) is ruled out for leased vehicles and for employer-provided vehicles.

The general format of page 2 is presented in Figure 10.1. As you will note, no line-by-line details are given. We want you to sense the formatting *functions*, rather than each line entry which may or may not apply.

Do note in Figure 10.1 that it accommodates two vehicles: Vehicle 1 and Vehicle 2. The implication is that if you are employed by two or more employers during the year, you may use different vehicles. Or, you may sell or trade one vehicle for another. Either way, you are instructed to use a separate column for each vehicle used for business during the year. You cannot lump several

MASTERING FORM 2106

Page 2 Part II	VEHICLE EXPENSES		Form 2106
Section A	General Information	Vehicle 1	Vehicle 2
Dates, mileages, and business use percentages (BUP)			
Questions on personal use and records kept			
Section B	Standard Mileage Rate	//////////	//////////
Cents per mile computations for total business miles on all vehicles (employee owned)			
Section C	Actual Expenses	Vehicle 1	Vehicle 2
Operating expenses, lease payments, value of employer-provided vehicle, depreciation (employee owned) from Section D			
Section D	Depreciation	*See instructions for limits*	
Vehicle 1	Business Use Portion Only ▶		
Vehicle 2	Business Use Portion Only ▶		
Cost or other basis, depreciation method and (cost recovery) percentage, limitation amount, and **the smaller of**.			

Fig. 10.1 - Functional Arrangement of Page 2, Form 2106: Vehicles

vehicles together and use only one column for all of your mileage and expense entries.

For each vehicle you must give the date (month/day/year) that it was "placed in service." Generally, this is the first date that you started using the vehicle for business purposes, even though you may have acquired it previously for personal purposes.

Important also is that you establish the BUP (business use percentage) of each vehicle that you "placed in service" on Form 2106. You do this as we discussed quite thoroughly in Chapter 7: Business Use of Auto. In fact, in Chapter 7 we covered the essentials of what you need for completing Section A (in Figure 10.1) on your own.

As to Section B: Standard Mileage Rate, we also touched on this in Chapter 7. It is an "optional method" useful only if you own

10-5

DEDUCTING JOB EXPENSES

(or are buying) your vehicle. If you do not use this method in he first year of vehicle service, you cannot use it in subsequent years. However, if you do use the standard mileage rate in the first year of service, you may switch to deducting actual expenses in the second or later years.

Actual Expense Entry Items

Section C: Actual Expenses (in Figure 10.1) is expanded in Figure 10.2. We have rearranged and simplified the numerous entry lines on the official form. We have done this to emphasize that Section C provides for entering expense items for three different vehicle ownership alternatives: (a) Employee owned vehicle, (b) Employee leased vehicle, and (c) Employer provided vehicle.

Page 2 Section C	ACTUAL EXPENSES	Form 2106	
		Vehicle 1	Vehicle 2
X	Gas, repairs, insurance, etc.		
(a)	Depreciation amount (from Section D)		
(b)	Rental payments (less inclusion amount)		
(c)	Employer-provided (annual lease value)		
Y	Add all of the above		
Z	Multiply **Y** by BUP		
Z^1	Add **Z** amounts for all vehicles; enter in Part I		

Fig. 10.2 - Rearrangement of Vehicle Expenses Required on Form 2106

Aside from operating expenses, each ownership alternative is allowed a deduction item that is characteristic of the ownership form. For Case (a), there is depreciation; for Case (b), there are rental payments; for Case (c), there is an annual lease value.

In all three cases, the first entry line in Section C requires that you summarize all actual (out-of-pocket) operating expenses. The official instructions to this entry line say—

MASTERING FORM 2106

Enter your total annual expenses for gasoline, oil, repairs, insurance, tires, license plates, or similar items. Do not include . . . interest expense you paid. Employees cannot deduct car loan interest.

If, instead of purchasing a vehicle, you leased it, the Form 2106 instructions say—

If you rented or leased a vehicle during the year instead of using one you own, enter the cost of renting. [However], *you have to reduce your deduction for lease payments by an amount called the* **inclusion amount**.

In the case of an employer-provided vehicle, generally you get no added deduction (beyond your operating expenses). The only exception is where your employer includes 100% of the vehicle's annual lease value in Box 1 of your W-2. If he includes *less* than 100%, it means that he has "factored out" your BUP portion of its business use, leaving only your personal-use portion in your W-2.

Section D: Depreciation of Vehicles (in Figure 10.1) applies only when you own the vehicle that you use for business. As we explained previously in Chapter 7, there are stringent depreciation limits on the business use of autos [IRC Sec. 280F(a)]. These limitations are listed in the official instructions to Form 2106. After multiplying the designated limitation amount by your BUP, the last line entry in Section D tells you to use the **smaller** of—

(i) the BUP limitation amount, or
(ii) your BUP depreciation amount.

All passenger vehicles and light trucks or vans are required to be depreciated over five years.

The applicable Section D amount is then added to your BUP amount of operating expenses in Section C. The last line entry on Section C tells you to total your allowable vehicle expenses for direct entry on the first line on page 1/Part I.

DEDUCTING JOB EXPENSES

Overview of Page 1/Part I

Below the title of Form 2106, there is headspace for your name, social security number, and occupation. The space for giving your occupation reads—

Occupation in which expenses were incurred.

The implication intended is that, if you worked for more than one employer during the year, in the same occupation, only one Form 2106 is necessary. Consequently, when characterizing your occupation for Form 2106 purposes, choose words that imply a whole raft of expenses in connection with that occupation.

If you are married, and your spouse is also working (whether for the same employer as you or not), the word "occupation" means that you each prepare separately your own Form 2106. When using two spousal Forms 2106, you distinguish between them by hand-entering the capitalized letters (**H**) and (**W**) prominently in the white space at the top of each respective Form 2106.

A synoptic overview of page 1/Part I is presented in Figure 10.3. As we did in Figure 10.1 (for page 2), we have intentionally omitted the official line entry details. Again, we want you to sense mostly the format and functions involved.

Particularly note in Figure 10.3 that Columns A and B are labeled as shown on the official Form 2106. It is not until you get down to line 9 that the real reason for the two columns emerges. You are instructed to start separating the columnar differences at lines 3 and 4.

In Step 1, lines 1 through 4 read officially as follows:

1. *Vehicle expenses from* [Part II].
2. *Parking fees, tolls, and transportation, including train, bus, etc., that **did not** involve overnight travel.*
3. *Travel expenses while away from home overnight, including lodging, airplane, car rentals, etc.* ***Do not*** *include meals and entertainment.*
4. *Business expenses not included on lines 1 through 3.* ***Do not*** *include meals and entertainment.*

MASTERING FORM 2106

Fig. 10.3 - General Format and Overview of Page 1, Form 2106

Page 1, Part I — EMPLOYEE BUSINESS EXPENSES — Form 2106		
Step 1 Your Expenses	Column A Other than M & E	Column B M & E Only
1 Vehicle(s), transportation, travel, lodging, and other related business expenses.	▓▓▓	▓▓▓
2		▓▓▓
3		▓▓▓
4 **Do not include any meals and entertainment (M & E) in Column A.**		▓▓▓
5	▓▓▓	
6 Total Expenses ▶		
Step 2 Reimbursements	▓▓▓▓▓▓	
7 Not reported in Box 1 of Form W-2		
Step 3 Net Expenses	▓▓▓▓▓▓	
8 See Text		
9	▓▓▓	
10 Transferable Expenses ▶		

↑ 2 1/2" White Space ↓

Lines 2 and 3 are reasonably self-explanatory. Note the emphasis in lines 3 and 4; note the emphasis on: *Do not include meals and entertainment* (M & E). This is because line 5 is reserved strictly for M & E. The instructions to line 5 say—

> *Include meals while away from your tax home overnight and other meals and business entertainment. Instead of actual cost, you may be able to claim the "standard meal allowance" for your daily meals and incidental expenses while away from your tax home overnight. Under this method, you deduct a specified*

DEDUCTING JOB EXPENSES

amount, depending on where you travel, instead of keeping records of your actual meal expenses.

With regard to the above-cited "standard meal allowance," keep in mind that it applies **only** to travel away from home overnight. Furthermore, it requires travel-point to travel-point reference to those CONUS and OCONUS per diem IRS tables described in Chapter 9.

General Business Expenses (Line 4)

Line 4/Step 1/Part I of Form 2106 is intended for ALL general business expenses that are not included in lines 1, 2, 3, and 5. In other words, line 4 *excludes* such items as: (a) vehicle expenses, (b) local transportation, (c) travel and lodging, and (d) meals and entertainment. Everything else — and we do mean EVERYTHING else that is a job-related expenditure — goes on line 4. This is a tall order.

The instructions to line 4 say—

Enter other job-related expenses not listed on any other line of this form. Include expenses for business gifts, education (tuition and books), home office, trade publications, etc. . . . If you are deducting depreciation or claiming a section 179 deduction on a cellular telephone or similar telecommunications equipment, a home computer, etc., get **Form 4562**, *Depreciation and Amortization, to figure the depreciation and section 179 deduction. Enter the depreciation and section 179 deduction on line 4. . . . Do not include expenses for . . . taxes or interest. Deductible taxes and interest are entered on . . . Schedule A.*

> *Editorial Note*: All line 4 matters on depreciation and the Section 179 deduction will be covered in Chapter 11: Depreciation Deductions (explaining Form 4562).

The problem with line 4 is that it covers the broadest possible range of job-related expenditures. So broad, in fact, that most IRS agents and examiners will not understand why some jobs and some job sites require unique expenditures and items out-of-the-ordinary.

MASTERING FORM 2106

To minimize potential dispute with the IRS, careful recordkeeping is required on *each category* of expenditures that you enter as part of the summary amount on line 4.

For whatever amount you enter on line 4, we don't see how you can avoid detailed backup on such expenditures as—

1. Union & professional dues
2. Books & publications
3. Educational courses
4. Seminars & updates
5. Entry fees to trade shows
6. Office/computer supplies
7. Small hand tools
8. Small business gifts
9. Display samples
10. Protective clothing
11. Uniforms & accessories
12. Telephone charges
13. Cellular phone service
14. Computer depreciation
15. Other equipment deprec.
16. Home office expenses
17. Home office deprec.
18. Storage space rental
19. Equipment rentals
20. Etc., Etc., Etc.

At the bottom of page 1, Form 2106, there is approximately 2 1/2" of vertical white space, running full-width of the page We suggest using this white space to type in, or hand-print in, an itemized listing of the expenses that you summarize in line 4. Use a bold asterisk (*) or some other identifying symbol for flagging line 4 to your listings in the white space. You can also add other notations such as See Statement; See Form 4562; See Worksheet, etc. There is ample white space for these notations.

The Reimbursement Quandary (Step 2)

Line 6, **Total expenses** in Step 1 is self-explanatory. You add together all of the line entries in Column A, and re-enter the single amount in Column B. You then go to line 7 which, in and of itself, comprises Step 2. Do not be fooled by the single line, two columns in Step 2. Here is where a lot of confusion arises. Step 2 (Columns A and B in Figure 10.3) consists solely of those reimbursements paid to you which are NOT included in Box 1 of your W-2. Let us explain.

First off, there is a little headnote above the Step 2 instruction which reads—

DEDUCTING JOB EXPENSES

Note: If you were not reimbursed for any expenses in step 1, skip line 7 and enter the amount from line 6 on line 8.

This sounds simple enough. But, what is meant by "not reimbursed" if your employer enters some or all of your reimbursements in Box 1 of your Form W-2?

Believe this or not: An expense reimbursement in Box 1 of your W-2 is NOT treated as a reimbursement for Form 2106 purposes! It is not treated as such because it is W-2 treated as "other compensation" . . . FULLY TAXABLE.

If there is reimbursement in Box 1 of your W-2, you DO NOT enter it again on line 7 of your Form 2106. To enter it again would have the effect of doubly taxing your reimbursement, by unwittingly reducing your deductible expenses. If reported in Box 1, and you are given no other reimbursement, you leave line 7 blank.

That which you enter in line 7 is that amount which your employer gave you which is NOT reported in Box 1 of your Form W-2. On this point, line 7 officially reads as follows:

*Enter amounts your employer gave you that were **not** reported to you in Box 1 of Form W-2. Include any amount reported under Code "L" in Box 13 of your Form W-2 (see instructions).*

The "see instructions" part refers to—

Amounts reported under Code "L" are certain reimbursements you received for business expenses that were not included as wages on Form W-2 because the expenses were treated as meeting specific IRS substantiation requirements.

Code "L" on your W-2 (Box 13) serves as a flashing light. It is your opportunity not to claim on Form 2106 those expenses that already have been deemed substantiated. But if you do claim them, you have to back out the Code "L" amount, so that you'll not get a double deduction benefit.

Otherwise, anything and everything that your employer gives you for expenses in Step 1 (that are not in Box 1 of your W-2) become an entry in line 7. This is why, in Chapter 9 we insisted that

MASTERING FORM 2106

you keep a cumulative record of all reimbursements made to you during the year.

Allocating Your Reimbursements

Technically, as you are reimbursed throughout the year, you should keep separate cumulative records of your Column A and Column B amounts. Raraely is this ever done. After submitting each expense voucher, most employers will reimburse you in *one check*. They simply will not issue two checks: one for M & E and one for non-M & E. Surely you can appreciate the added paperwork to your employer — and to yourself — if you submitted 5, 10, or 15 expense vouchers during the year. You'd be doing better than the average employee by just keeping a cumulative total on all reimbursements received.

Consequently, a unique problem arises with respect to Line 7/Form 2106. Assuming that you have one grand total for all of your reimbursements for the year, how do you make entry into the "two-box" line 7 amounts?

This is where the reimbursement *allocation rule* comes into play. This rule is stated in the instructions, as follows:

> *If your employer paid you a single amount that covers both meals and entertainment, as well as other business expenses, you must allocate the reimbursement so that you know how much to enter in Column A and Column B of line 7.*

The instructions provide a 6-step worksheet for making the allocation. The allocation essence is that you first establish an M & E fraction (MEF) from the total expenses in line 6, Columns A and B. That is, your MEF is

$$\frac{\text{Col. B, line 6}}{(\text{Col. A} + \text{Col. B}), \text{line 6}}$$

decimalized to at least two places. For example, suppose your Column A, line 6 amount is $10,500 and your Column B, line 6 amount is $2,500. Your M & E fraction would become

10-13

DEDUCTING JOB EXPENSES

$$\text{MEF} = \frac{2,500}{10,500 + 2,500} = \frac{2,500}{13,000} = 0.1923$$

Suppose, now, that your total reimbursement for the year (not in Box 1 of Form W-2) is $6,780. How much is your M & E reimbursement for the Column B box of line 7? How much is your non-M & E entry for the Column A box of line 7?

Answers:

Col. B = $6,780 × 0.1923 = $1,304
Col. A = $6,780 × [1 − 0.1923] = 5,476

Total reimbursement = $6,780

Lines 6, 7, and 8 comprise the "tricky part" of Form 2106. Within these three lines lies the whole source of confusion regarding what an employer reimburses and does not reimburse. Understanding the role of these three lines is the key to optimum Form 2106 preparation. Hopefully, Figure 10.4 helps you to better understand the importance of these lines. Be fully aware that an entry at line 7 consists **only** of those reimbursed amounts which are **not** already included in Box 1 of your Form W-2.

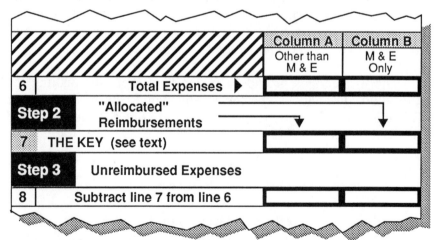

Fig. 10.4 - The "Tricky Part" (Expenses Less Reimbursements) of Form 2106

MASTERING FORM 2106

What If "Excess" Reimbursement?

The basic premise of Form 2106 is that your job-related expenses, when entered on the form, generally exceed your reimbursements. The idea is that you total separately Columns A and B, then subtract your allocated A and B reimbursements. You wind up with a net amount in each column which becomes your net (tentative) deductible expenses.

Using the example figures above, we have the following scenario:

	Col. A	Col. B	Col. A + B
Totaled expenses	$10,500	$2,500	$13,000
Allocated reimbursement	<5,476>	<1,304>	<6,780>
Tentatively deductible	$ 5,024	$ 1,196	$ 6,220

Suppose the figures above were reversed. That is, your Column A + B expenses were $6,780 and your Column A + B reimbursements were $13,000. What happens in this case?

The initial obvious answer is that you have *excess* reimbursement. The amount of this excess (using the reversed figures above) would be $6,220. What do you do with this excess amount of reimbursement? Do you pocket it as "free money"?

In no way! Surely, you must know that the IRS would not let you pocket any "free money" from your employer. You have to report it as **income** on your Form 1040. You report it as additional *Wages, salaries, tips, etc.* in the income section on page 1 of Form 1040. This is what invariably happens when you inadvertently add the reimbursements **in** Box 1 of your W-2 to the reimbursements **not in** Box 1.

Except for inadvertency, excess reimbursement to an ordinary employee is very rare. When it happens, it usually applies to owner-employees, top executives, or key marketers who are favored with "open-ended" expense accounts and car allowances. Even though rare, the potential for over-reimbursement to key employees is the very reason why the IRS keeps trying to force employers to put most reimbursements in Box 1 of Form W-2.

DEDUCTING JOB EXPENSES

The Line 9, Column B Clincher

Step 3 of Form 2106 carries the instructional heading:

Figure Expenses to Deduct on Schedule A (Form 1040)

The Step 3 block consists of lines 8, 9, and 10, as previously depicted in Figure 10.3. Lines 8 and 9 each are continuations of Columns A and B. Line 10 is a single-columnar box which totals the two residuals in Column A and Column B on line 9.

Line 8 is officially identified as—

Subtract line 7 from line 6

The results of the subtraction are tentative deductible amounts. There is a Column A tentative amount and a Column B tentative amount. Both of these appear on line 8.

Line 9 becomes the clincher. It is the sole and only reason why Form 2106 is formatted into two separate columns: A and B. Column B, recall, is the M & E column.

There are two separate entry instructions for line 9. They are:

(1) In Column A, enter the amount from line 8 (if zero or less, enter -0-).
(2) In Column B, **multiply** the amount on line 8 by 50% (0.50). [Emphasis added.]

Do you see the clincher? It is Column B, line 9: 50%. In other words, after all of your Column B effort for M & E, you **lose 50%** of your net M & E expenses after reimbursement! Apparently, the IRS and Congress figure that you'd be living too high on the hog if they were to allow 100% of your bona fide business meals and entertainment costs.

The 50% M & E Law

What Form 2106, line 9, Column B derives from — though totally silent on the form itself — is Section 274(n)(1) of the IR

Code. This section is titled: *Only 50 Percent of Meal and Entertainment Expenses Allowed as Deduction.* We don't know what could be more punitive and specific than this. The vindictive attitude behind this section tempts many M & E spenders to intentionally pad their non-M & E expenses to make up for their direct, out-of-pocket M & E losses.

Section 274(n)(1) reads essentially in full as:

The amount allowable as a deduction for—

(A) any expense for food or beverages, and
(B) any item with respect to an activity which is of a type generally considered to constitute entertainment, amusement, or recreation . . .
shall not exceed 50 percent of the amount of such expense or item which would (but for this paragraph) be allowable as a deduction.

Paragraph (2) of Section 274(n) provides for a menu of exceptions to the 50% M & E loss rule. The exceptions are those where the M & E expenditures are:

1. Included as compensation on an employee's W-2.
2. Furnished on employer's premises for his convenience, such as to firefighters, merchant seamen, and 24-hour duty personnel.
3. Included in a "package ticket" such as air fares, seminar fees, and box-lunch affairs.
4. De minimis fringe benefits, such as coffee, soft drinks, and sweet rolls provided by employer.

In reality, the above-type exceptions are not really relevant to Form 2106, and, therefore, the form is silent with respect to them.

The 50% M & E loss rule applies after all other M & E limitation rules (such as "not lavish or extravagant") have been met. It is for this reason that the 50% M & E loss appears in the next-to-last entry line on Form 2106.

DEDUCTING JOB EXPENSES

Last Item on Form 2106

As previously indicated (in Figure 10.3), line 10 is the very last entry line on Part I of Form 2106. It is a single-entry box combining the residuals of Columns A and B from line 9. The first instruction at line 10 says—

> *Add the amounts on line 9 of both columns and enter the total here.*

Thus, once you arrive at line 10, there is no distinction between M & E and non-M & E matters. From this point on, all expenses are treated the same.

In addition, at line 10, there is a bold-printed instruction which reads—

> ***Also enter the total on Schedule A (Form 1040), line 20.***

What this instruction is telling you is to transfer the line 10 amount to a designated line number on Schedule A (1040). For 1996, the designated line number on Schedule A is Line 20.

Schedule A (1040), you may recall, is titled: ***Itemized Deductions***. The designated transfer line is headed:

> *Unreimbursed employee expenses — job travel, union dues, job education, etc. If required, you **MUST** attach Form 2106.*

The Schedule A designated line number may change from year to year, so follow the transfer instructions carefully. If you transfer the line 10/Form 2106 amount to the wrong line number on Schedule A (1040), the IRS's computer will zap you. Its computer may even disallow the transferred amount altogether.

11

DEPRECIATION DEDUCTIONS

> Property Items — Vehicles, Furniture, Tools, Computers, Telecom Devices, And Other Equipment — Purchased For Business Use Are Allowed Certain Depreciation Deductions Over Defined (Cost) Recovery Periods. Special Recapture And Straight-Line-Only Rules Apply When Business Use Drops To 50% Or Less. Other Than Auto Depreciation (Calculated On Form 2106), All MACRS Depreciation And Section 179 Deductions For The Placement-In-Service Year Are Computed On Form 4562. For Subsequent-Year Deductions, The Form 4562 DEPRECIATION WORKSHEET Is Used. This Becomes Your "Permanent Record" . . . Until The Items Are Disposed Of.

Depreciation is a tax allowance for the wear, tear, exhaustion, and obsolescence of tangible property used in business. It is a way of recovering one's capital cost of acquiring and owning business property. The recovery allowance is a "capital expense" deduction in contrast to ordinary operating/consumption-type expense deductions.

The depreciation rules apply equally to employers and employees. Whoever buys the property, and puts it to business use, gets an annual depreciation deduction for it. However, there is a key difference between employer purchases and employee purchases. Employers tend to use the property 100% in business. Employees rarely can claim legitimately 100% business use. More often than not, an employee's business use is less — sometimes

DEDUCTING JOB EXPENSES

considerably less — than 100%. When it is, the statutory depreciation allowance has to be modified by the employee's BUP (business use percentage) portion of the item.

Technically, any tangible property item costing more than $100, and used in business more than one year, is tax classed as *depreciable property*. This means that its cost recovery has to be stretched out over its useful business life. Furthermore, the stretching-out process has to be cumulatively tracked throughout the depreciation recovery years. Most employees are not familiar with this kind of expense recordkeeping nor the subtleties of the depreciation rules.

Consequently, in this chapter we want to familiarize you with the depreciation deduction process, depreciation methods, and depreciation recapture rules that are most applicable to the type of property items that you would most likely buy and use for your employer's business. We also want to familiarize you with the special depreciation election option you have as a "small business" person: statutorily known as "The Section 179 Election."

Recovery Classes: Employee Property

Over the years, one of the most contentious areas of tax law has been determining the recovery periods for depreciable property. Contentions and disputes arose because the IRS insisted on applying the "determinable useful life" concept. This concept means that, if an item of property doesn't physically disintegrate and disengage from use on its own, it has prolonged useful life, including salvage value. In 1986, Congress started changing the IRS's attitude and is continuing to do so to this date. Instead of old-fashioned-type depreciation, there is now what is called: MACRS depreciation. (MACRS = Modified Accelerated Cost Recovery System.)

Under MACRS, all forms of tangible property (except real estate) are statutorily assigned to six recovery-period classes. Real estate is assigned three recovery classes: residential, nonresidential, and railroad gradings/tunnel bores. All nine recovery classes are prescribed by IRC Section 168(e): *Classification of Property*. These are mandatory classes, which the IRS cannot tinker with and stretch out endlessly.

DEPRECIATION DEDUCTIONS

Once an item of property fits within a statutory class, full recovery of one's capital cost of that property is allowed. Salvage value, if any, is tax treated as zero. For a statutory cost recovery period, a "year" is a 12-month period. It is not a calendar year.

For employees, other than office-in-home real estate, there are three recovery classes that are most pertinent. These are 3-year, 5-year, and 7-year properties. We show in Figure 11.1 the types of items likely to be purchased by employees and used for business purposes. Here, the term "for business purposes" includes the trade or business of one's employer (Sec. 162) as well as maintaining and improving skills in an employee's chosen occupation (Sec. 212).

	RECOVERY CLASS	CLASS LIFESPAN	EXAMPLES
(1)	3 year	4 yrs. or less	Power tools, dies, jigs, R&D items, computer software, carts & trays
(2)	5 year	4 to 10 yrs.	Autos, light trucks, computers; telecom; equipment: office, shop, medical
(3)	7 year	10 to 16 yrs.	Furniture, fixtures, & furnishings; heavy duty trucks, machinery, equip.

Fig. 11.1 - Employee-Likely Purchases for Cost Recovery Purposes

It is instructive to point out that the statutory definition of 5-year property [Subsection 168(e)(3)(B)] includes—

(iv) any qualified technological equipment,

Qualified technological equipment is further defined in Subsection 168(i)(2)(A) as—

(i) any computer or peripheral equipment,
(ii) any high technology telephone equipment installed on the customer's premises, and
(iii) any high technology medical equipment.

The term "computer or peripheral equipment" shall not include—

DEDUCTING JOB EXPENSES

> (I) *any equipment which is an integral part of other property which is not a computer,*
> (II) *typewriters, calculators, adding and accounting machines, copiers, duplicating equipment, and similar equipment and*
> (III) *equipment of a kind used primarily for amusement or entertainment of the user.*

Except for computer software and furniture/furnishings, most electronic, telecom, and office equipment purchased by employees would fall in the 5-year-property category.

MACRS Methods & Conventions

The general tax rule for depreciation deductions is Section 167(a). It reads in essential part as—

There shall be allowed as a depreciation deduction a reasonable allowance for . . .

> *(1) property used in a trade or business* [Sec. 162], *or*
> *(2) property held for the production of income* [Sec. 212].

The MACRS general rule, Section 168(a), says (in part)—

The depreciation deduction provided by section 167(a) for any tangible property shall be determined by using—

> *(1) the applicable depreciation method,*
> *(2) the applicable recovery period, and*
> *(3) the applicable convention.*

We've already touched on the applicable recovery period for property items likely to be purchased by employees. We need now to address depreciation methods and applicable conventions.

Section 168(b) describes the applicable depreciation methods as:

A. 200% declining balance [200 DB], switching to straight line,

DEPRECIATION DEDUCTIONS

B. 150% declining balance [150 DB], switching to straight line,
C. Straight line [S/L].

The "switching to straight line" means the first taxable year for which using the straight-line method will yield the larger allowance. Rather than each employee figuring this out for himself, the IRS has published recovery percentage tables. We summarize these IRS tables for you in Figure 11.2.

MACRS DEPRECIATION METHODS (HY) *

Recovery Period		200 DB	150 DB	S/L
3 yrs.	1	33.33%	25.00%	16.67%
	2	44.45%	37.50%	33.33%
	3	14.81%	18.75%	33.33%
	4	7.41%	18.75%	16.67%
5 yrs.	1	20.00%	15.00%	10.00%
	2	32.00%	25.50%	20.00%
	3	19.20%	17.85%	20.00%
	4	11.52%	16.66%	20.00%
	5	11.52%	16.66%	20.00%
	6	5.76%	8.33%	10.00%
7 yrs.	1	14.29%	10.71%	7.14%
	2	24.49%	19.13%	14.28%
	3	17.49%	15.03%	14.29%
	4	12.49%	12.25%	14.28%
	5	8.93%	12.25%	14.29%
	6	8.92%	12.25%	14.28%
	7	8.93%	12.25%	14.29%
	8	4.46%	6.13%	7.15%

★ (HY) = Half-Year Convention. The 1st year is always a "half-year". Thus, the last year is always a half-year beyond the designated recovery period.

Fig. 11.2 - Depreciation "Percentages" for Employee Recovery Periods

DEDUCTING JOB EXPENSES

Section 168(d) describes the applicable conventions as:

(1) In General — the half-year (HY) convention
(2) Real Property — the mid-month (MM) convention
(3) Special Rule — the mid-quarter (MQ) convention

The half-year convention treats all property (other than real estate) placed in service during any taxable year (or disposed of during any taxable year) as placed in service (or disposed of) at the mid-point of such taxable year. This convention applies to *all* 3- to 20-year property, unless the MQ convention applies. Figure 11.2 is based on the HY convention.

The MQ (mid-quarter) convention applies when more than 40% of the purchased property is placed in service during the last three months of the taxable year. This is a drawback in that it requires that all property placed in service during the year be mid-quartered throughout the year, using the straight-line method. This adds computational complexity. The purpose of mid-quartering is to discourage buying substantial amounts of property in December, on the expectation of claiming half-year benefits. To avert this handicap, the obvious thing to do is to buy at least 60% of your property prior to October of any given year.

Now for "Listed Property"

Listed property is mixed-business-and-personal-use property. It is a type that is a "natural" for personal use under the guise of a business purpose. Statutorily, it is defined in Section 280F(d)(4) as—

> (A) ***In General***: *Except as provided in subparagraph (B), the term "listed property" means—*
> (i) *any passenger automobile*
> (ii) *any other property used as a means of transportation* [boats, airplanes, campers],
> (iii) *any property of a type generally used for purposes of entertainment, recreation, or amusement,*
> (iv) *any computer or peripheral equipment,*

DEPRECIATION DEDUCTIONS

(v) any cellular telephone (or other similar telecommunications equipment), and

(vi) any other property of the type specified by the [IRS] *by regulations.*

(B) Exception for Certain Computers: The term "listed property" shall not include any computer or peripheral equipment [on-line or off-line] **used exclusively at a regular business establishment** *and owned or leased by the person operating such establishment. Any portion of a dwelling unit shall be treated as a regular business establishment if (and only if) the requirements of section 280A(c)(1)* [Office-in-home rules] *are met with respect to such portion.* [Emphasis added.]

Paragraph (A) above is a broad swipe at those property items likely to be purchased by employees, that have a recreational or personal-use entertainment feature. By focusing on these items, special rules can be imposed to limit the depreciation allowances associated with such property.

Paragraph (B) provides a statutory exception to the limitation rules where it can be shown that "certain computers" (and their peripherals) are **used exclusively at** a regular place of business. Such a place of business may be at the employer's premises or at the employee's premises, so long as either qualifies as a "business establishment." An example of the "certain computer" distinction is that of a desktop computer versus a laptop computer. The ease of portability of a laptop computer ascribes to it the potential of being an entertainment device for children and other members of an employee's family. In contrast, a desktop computer can be loaded with business-use only software, left in place, where access is denied to nonemployee users.

Listed Property Limitations

Listed property is an entirely separate classification of property apart from Section 168(e) for recovery periods. It is a carving out from the general depreciation rules certain property on which

DEDUCTING JOB EXPENSES

limitations can be imposed. Imposing limitations on depreciation is an area where the IRS just loves to stir the pot.

In broad terms, there are three avenues for limiting an employee's depreciation of listed property. These avenues are:

One. The property must be required by, or be for, the express convenience of one's employer [Sec. 280F(d)(3)].

Two. The business use percentage (BUP) must be established **each year**, separately from all other prior use years [Sec. 280F(d)(6)].

Three. When business use falls to 50% or below for any year, there is **recapture** of excess depreciation over straight line for all prior years [Sec. 280F(b)(2)].

A few words about each of these limitations is in order.

The depreciation deduction for listed property is not something that one can take for granted. Your assertion alone that a property item has a business use or need is not good enough. As an employee you need some form of statement, assurance, or policy pronouncement from your employer that he knows of, approves, requires, or agrees with you that the item (or items) purchased serve a bona fide business purpose. The common thread for legitimacy is "condition of employment" or "for convenience of employer." Sometimes, an employee's official job description (in writing) will meet the common thread on its own. But not always.

For example, small employers may not be willing to pay for ergonomic chairs, keyboards, and workstations for employees who are subject to the RSI (repetitive stress injury) or CT (carpal tunnel) syndromes. Such employers are sympathetic to the need, but cannot afford the high cost of providing custom-designed furniture and equipment to every employee. Instead, such employers will encourage and permit those employees who wish to do so to procure their own property items for employer-certified business use. When this is the case, some corroborating statement from one's employer is essential.

DEPRECIATION DEDUCTIONS

Ordinarily, when one buys any item of business property with any mixed use, he establishes a BUP for that item. Ordinarily, also, the BUP is constant year after year, throughout the statutory cost-recovery period. This is particularly true of property used predominantly in business: meaning more than 50%. In the case of listed property, however, the BUP has to be established **each year**. There is no presumption or automatic acceptance that it is the same use percentage each year. Re-establishing the BUP each year adds complications to one's cumulative depreciation recordkeeping, no doubt about it. But you must do this if you want the tax benefits of the accelerated depreciation methods: 200 DB or 150 DB.

The real target of the limitation rules is **depreciation recapture**. That is, if your BUP falls to 50% or below, all depreciation taken in excess of straight line is recaptured for all prior years. This is so prescribed by Section 280F(b)(2): *Recapture where business use percentage does not exceed 50 percent*. For example, suppose your MACRS depreciation for a prior year was $2,000 based on 60% business use (when the corresponding straight line depreciation would have been, say, $1,200). Your current year business use falls to 40%. The excess prior depreciation (2,000 − 1,200 = 800) is recaptured as ordinary income, after which your current and subsequent years' depreciation is based on the S/L method times your BUP each year. Recapture is an income penalty for aggressively using MACRS depreciation for listed property.

The Section 179 Election

Section 179 of the IR Code is titled: *Election to Expense Certain Depreciable Business Assets*. This is a special rule under special conditions by which a taxpayer — employer or employee — can elect to expense certain property items without depreciating them under the MACRS rules. Up to a prescribed amount, the cost of the property does not have to be prorated from the date of placement in service to the end of the year. Even if purchased in December, and placed in service then, the entire purchase cost (up to the prescribed maximum) can be one-time expensed. Of course, there are some catches and pitfalls. But, first, let's quote the pertinent parts of the statutory language on point.

DEDUCTING JOB EXPENSES

Section 179(a): *Treatment as Expenses*, is the general rule. It reads in full as—

A taxpayer may elect to treat the cost of any section 179 property as an expense which is not chargeable to capital account. Any cost so treated shall be allowed as a deduction for the taxable year in which the property is placed in service.

Thus, except for listed property and passenger autos, one could purchase certain business property items and expense them — and recover the full cost — in the year of purchase. This is because, under Section 179(a), there is no applicable 3-, 5-, or 7-year cost-recovery period as referenced in Figures 11.1 and 11.2.

The maximum prescribed amount for any one year . . . *shall not exceed . . . $25,000* [when "phased in" through year 2003; **see page 11-18** for the year-to-year phase-in schedule]. For employees and small business owners, this is a comfortably adequate amount. However, the purchased item must be tangible property used in the **active conduct** of a trade or business [Sec. 179(d)(1)]. Regulation 1.179-2(c)(6)(iv) states that—

Employees are considered to be engaged in the active conduct of the trade or business of their employment.

Introduction to Form 4562

When claiming a depreciation deduction for business-use property, an employee's first resort is Form 2106: *Employee Business Expenses*. A close examination of this form reveals that it addresses the depreciation computation for **vehicles only**. (Recall Figure 10.1.) If one has purchased other than vehicle 3-, 5-, or 7-year-recovery property, where does he compute and claim his depreciation?

Answer: **Form 4562**. This form is titled: *Depreciation and Amortization (Including Information on Listed Property)*.

Form 4562 is a two-page form with nearly 60 different entry lines, and nearly 30 different columnar headings. It is too complicated to abridge and functionalize as we did for Form 2106.

DEPRECIATION DEDUCTIONS

This is because Form 4562 is designed for use by all types of businesses: proprietorships, partnerships, and corporations. It can accommodate employees with business-use property, but it is not for employees only as is Form 2106.

Form 4562 is arranged in the following parts, with official headings as cited:

Part I — Election to Expense Certain Tangible Property (Section 179). (Note: If you have any "Listed Property," complete Part V before you complete Part I.)

Part II — MACRS Depreciation for Assets Placed in Service ONLY During Your [Current] Tax Year. (Do Not Include Listed Property.)

Part III — Other Depreciation. (Do Not Include Listed Property.)

Part IV — Summary

Part V — Listed Property — Automobiles, Certain Other Vehicles, Cellular Telephones, Certain Computers, and Property Used for Entertainment, Recreation, or Amusement.

Form 4562: Listed Property Portion

The IRS is intransigent on the listed property rules. It is the one area of depreciation deductions where it can beat an employee, self-employed, or small business owner into total submission to its disallowance power. The only way to survive is for an employee to thoroughly understand the distinction between listed and nonlisted property. When in doubt, treat it as listed property and proceed accordingly. If you don't, the IRS will.

Your listed property depreciation deductions go on Part V of For 4562. The leadoff instructions to Part V tell you that, if you are

DEDUCTING JOB EXPENSES

claiming depreciation on a passenger automobile and on no other listed property, you should use Form 2106. Otherwise—

> *You must provide the information requested in Part V, regardless of the year the property was placed in service.*

This means that each year you use the property for business purposes, you have to independently establish the BUP for that year. What this also means is: You cannot make a one-time election under Section 179 and cease reporting the property in its subsequent-use years. Once an item is characterized as listed property, it always stays as such, unless it meets the "exclusive business use" exception.

The depreciation computations in Part V of Form 4562 are unique in that you have to group the property items into (1) more-than-50%-use category, and (2) 50%-or-less-use category. Only for the more-than-50%-use category can you claim any Section 179 election, and/or MACRS 200 DB/150 DB depreciation. For the 50%-or-less category, you must use straight-line depreciation without any Section 179 election.

A rearrangement of the lines and columnar entries on Part V of Form 4562 is presented in Figure 11.3. We show the entry lines vertically — easier to read, we think — whereas the official form shows them horizontally. Except for minor editing (to reduce words), the entry line descriptions correspond with those on the official form. If you really want your listed property depreciation deduction, you'll have to work your way through the Figure 11.3 computational sequence. There is no magic wand that you can wave to do it for you.

Form 4562: The Section 179 Portion

Let us turn attention now to Part I of Form 4562: the Section 179 election. The instructions to this part say—

> *You must have purchased the property and placed it in service during the* [purchase] *year. . . . You must make the election with the original return you file for the tax year the property was*

DEPRECIATION DEDUCTIONS

Form 4562	LISTED PROPERTY DEPRECIATION		
Part V	Questions Regarding "Written Evidence"		
ITEM		More than 50%	50% or less
(a)	Description of property		
(b)	Date placed in service		
(c)	Business Use Percentage (%)		
(d)	Cost or other basis		
(e)	Basis: business depreciation	[multiply line (d) by line (c)]	
(f)	Recovery period (yrs) [Fig. 11.1]		
(g)	Depreciation method, % [Fig. 11.2]	S/L	S/L
(h)	Depreciation deduction	[multiply line (e) by % on line (g)]	
(i)	Section 179 election		/////
/////	Add all line (h) amounts; enter and transfer to Part IV: Summary		
/////	Add all line (i) amounts; enter and transfer to Part I: Sec. 179		

Fig. 11.3 - Entry Details for Depreciating Listed Property on Form 4562

*placed in service. . . . Once made, the election (and the selection of the property you elect to expense) may not be revoked without IRS consent. . . . Section 179 property does **not** include property used 50% or less in your trade or business, or property held for* [passive] *investment.*

The part I portion of Form 4562 consists of about 15 entry lines, many of which are not applicable to employees. Furthermore, the official form provides for a "carryover" — to the year after purchase

11-13

DEDUCTING JOB EXPENSES

— of any unallowable portion of the up to $25,000 election maximum, if due to purchases exceeding one's taxable income. We don't believe that any employee knowingly would purchase, for the convenience of his employer, property items costing more than his taxable wages for the year.

With the above comments in mind, we present in Figure 11.4 an edited/abbreviated version of Part I, Form 4562. Particularly note the *separate line* for listed property brought forward from part V. This "bringing forward" of the Section 179 election emphasizes the fact that Part I is intended for nonlisted property or property of a type which is expressly excepted from the listed property rules.

Part I Form 4562	ELECTION TO EXPENSE CERTAIN TANGIBLE PROPERTY (Section 179)		
1	Maximum limitation [See page 11-18 for phase-ins]		$25,000
2	(a) Description of property	(b) Cost	(c) Elected cost
	Listed property amount from Part V		
	Total elected cost of Sec. 179 property		
3	Tentative deduction: SMALLER of lines 1 or 3		
4	Taxable income limitation (Box 1 of Form W-2)		
5	Allowable deduction: SMALLER of lines 4 or 5		
6	Transfer line 6 amount to Part IV: Summary		

Fig. 11.4 - Edited/Abbreviated Version of the Sec. 179 Expense Deduction

The instructions to Part V define the exceptions to listed property as:

> *Listed property does **not** include (a) photographic, phonographic, communication, or video equipment **used exclusively** in a taxpayer's trade or business or at the taxpayer's regular business establishment; or (b) any computer or peripheral equipment **used exclusively** at a regular business establishment and owned or leased by the person operating the establishment.* [Emphasis added.]

11-14

DEPRECIATION DEDUCTIONS

Otherwise, items that are statutorily not defined in Section 280F(d)(4) as listed property are automatically classed as nonlisted property. Characteristically, these are items which have little or no personal, family, or recreational-use likelihood. If, as an employee, you buy nonlisted items for job-necessity purposes, we urge that you use the Section 179 election to its fullest.

Form 4562: MACRS Portion

Part II of Form 4562 is devoted entirely to first-year MACRS depreciation. In other words, it is to be used **only** for the placement-in-service year. Furthermore, your entries here must not include any listed property. For years subsequent to the initial placement in service, you are expected to keep on separate worksheets the cumulative depreciation taken throughout all years of the statutory recovery periods.

If the only depreciable asset you have for business use is an automobile (or light van or pickup truck), you do not need Form 4562. You can handle the depreciation of two automobiles at a time on Form 2106. But, if you place in service any other property — listed or nonlisted — you will need, and must have, Form 4562. After the year of placement in service, you still have to record and compute the annual depreciation deduction for each subsequent year throughout each property's recovery period.

This is where the *Depreciation Worksheet* in the Form 4562 instructions comes in handy.

For your preview and edification, the Form 4562 Depreciation Worksheet consists of the following columnar headings:

1. Description of property
2. Date placed in service
3. Cost or other basis
4. Business use %
5. Section 179 deduction
6. Depreciation prior years
7. Basis for depreciation
8. Method/convention
9. Recovery period
10. Rate or table %
11. Depreciation deduction

You assign a separate line for each different property item that you are depreciating. At the end of each current year, show a subtotal

11-15

DEDUCTING JOB EXPENSES

for that year. The single subtotal is then transferred to Part III of Form 4562, with the notation: "See Worksheet."

Although referred to as a "worksheet," the Form 4562 Depreciation Worksheet is tax classed as a *permanent record*. Once you associate the concept of records permanency with this full page, 11 column, **36** line, IRS-designed format, you'll sense many other uses for it. The 36 horizontal lines provide ample space for permanently recording every conceivable property item you use in business as an employee.

Office-in-Home Depreciation

If applicable, the most worthwhile use of your worksheet has to do with your office-in-home (if you own the home). As we discussed in Chapter 8: Business Use of Home, you prepare a little sketch showing the office space and overall home dimensions. From these figures, you establish your BUP. For permanent record purposes, you can enter the square footages and BUP in the lower portion of your worksheet. Do this in a way that does not interfere with your *active* depreciation schedules (for Part II of Form 4562).

Also, in the lower portion of the worksheet, enter your County Assessor's data for the value of your home: land and improvement (building structure). This enables you to show computation of the fraction of your home that is building structure. It is this structure that depreciates: not the land to which it is attached. For example, suppose the assessor's data shows the following:

```
Land            $27,450 )
                        )    Total = $100,815
Improvement     $73,365 )
```

What would your building structure fraction be?

Answer: $\dfrac{73,365}{100,815} = 0.7277 \approx 73\%$

This fraction times your total acquisition cost, times your office BUP, is the amount of office structure that is depreciable over a 30-

DEPRECIATION DEDUCTIONS

year cost recovery period. There is absolutely no provision on Form 2106 or Form 4562 to post and retain office-in-home depreciation computations. But, you *can* make such provision on your permanent worksheet.

Transference to Form 2106

The summary portion of Form 4562: Part IV, consists of one "bottom line." This is the line labeled: **Total**. This one line is the grand total of all subtotals of the various parts of the form. The preprinted instruction at the grand total line says—

> *Add deductions on lines _____ through _____.*
> *Enter here and on the appropriate lines of your return.*

This instruction is telling you to transfer your total depreciation deduction to some "appropriate line" on your return. As an employee, what line on what form or schedule would that be?

The form that you transfer to is **Form 2106**: Employee Business Expenses. But on what line do you make the entry?

Actually, on Form 2106 there is no direct entry line for transferring your depreciation from Form 4562. It becomes an *indirect* entry because the depreciation amount is combined with other miscellaneous business expenses on line 4 of Form 2106 (recall Figure 10.3). The instructions to line 4/Form 2106 say, in part—

> *If you are deducting home office* [depreciation] *... or deducting* [other] *depreciation or claiming a section 179 deduction on a cellular telephone, telecommunications equipment, home computer, etc., get* ***Form 4562*** *... to figure* [your] *deduction. Enter the depreciation and section 179 deduction on line 4.*

If you recall our Chapter 10, line 4/Form 2106 is a conglomeration of all your business expenses that are not required entries on lines 1 (vehicle expenses), 2 (local transportation), 3 (travel & lodging), and 5 (meals & entertainment). This "conglomeration" is why we encouraged you to itemize all of your

11-17

DEDUCTING JOB EXPENSES

line 4 expenses in that 2^{1}/$_{2}$" (vertical) white space at the bottom of page 1 of Form 2106. In your itemizing process, designate a separate item as:

Depreciation: Form 4562 $ _____

Also, in the white space, show the total of your items listed. This total, then, is what is entered at line 4.

From this point on, your depreciation deduction combines with all other business expenses on line 4 of Form 2106. After making those subtractions which we covered in Chapter 10, you arrive at a "tentative" total Form 2106 deduction amount. This tentative amount is transferred to still another tax form, namely: Schedule A (Form 1040).

Editorial Note: The $25,000 Section 179 expense election "phases in" as follows—

Taxable year	Applicable amount
1997	$18,000
1998	18,500
1999	19,000
2000	20,000
2001, 2002	24,000
2003 or thereafter	25,000

Ref: IRC Sec. 179(b)(1).

12

SCHEDULE A (1040) WRAP-UP

> The Net Total On Form 2106 Is Transferred To Schedule A At Line: UNREIMBURSED EMPLOYEE EXPENSES. There It Combines With Other Miscellaneous Deductions To Be Subjected To A Subtraction Amount Equal To 2% Of Your AGI. After Surpassing The "Standard Deduction," There Is A Further Subtraction Of 3% Of Your AGI In Excess Of $100,000. After Determining Your Tax The Regular Way, Your Job Expenses — Along With Other Benefits, Savings, And Preferences — Are ADDED BACK For Determining Your AMT Tax. Despite These Limitations, Your Out-Of-Pocket Job Expenses Are COST OF EARNING INCOME . . . Which Is Deductible.

Except for moving expenses (Chapter 6), all other job-related expenses that you incur for business purposes (Chapters 3, 4, 5, 7, 8, 9, 11) go on Form 2106. We tried to emphasize to you the importance of this form in Chapter 10. The net bottom line amount claimed on Form 2106 is then transferred to Schedule A (Form 1040). On Schedule A, there are other subtractions and adjustments that serve to whittle down the net/net deductions that you can ultimately take. We're certainly going to tell you in this chapter about all of the whittling-down steps involved.

There was a time (prior to 1987), when Form 2106 employee business expenses were directly deductible against one's total income on page 1 of Form 1040: U.S. Individual Income Tax Return. This put Form 2106 on a par with IRA deductions, Keogh

DEDUCTING JOB EXPENSES

retirement plans, and self-employed SEP plans. This meant that Form 2106 was a direct dollar-for-dollar offset against your other sources of income. But, no more.

In one of the great brainstorms of the decade, the IRS came up with an idea for reducing the effectiveness of Form 2106. It urged Congress to require that Form 2106 be folded into Schedule A where it could be subjected to a 2% AGI "qualifying threshold." The IRS posed this idea as part of its ongoing effort under the Paperwork Reduction Act. This is the type of tax gimmick that Congress loves. It was a brilliant way to increase revenues . . . without increasing taxes. Congress loved the idea so much that it enacted a special section of the tax code — namely, Section 67 — in its Tax Reform Act of 1986. We'll quote this section to you, later.

In the meantime, our focus in this, our final chapter, is to show how Schedule A, with Form 2106 included in it, fits into the computational sequence for arriving at your tax. You must go through the sequence if you want any deduction benefits from the job expenses you incurred. True, some added complications are involved. But, if you want the tax deductions that you are entitled to, you have to do the homework that you are required to do. Using the EZ and "short forms" is no way to reduce your tax.

Overall Role of Schedule A

There was also a time (prior to 1987) when Schedule A was THE primary source of deductions for all individual taxpayers: employed, unemployed, nonemployed, and self-employed alike. It truly was the springboard for significant tax deduction benefits. This, among other reasons, is why it was (still is) officially titled: *Itemized Deductions — Attach to Form 1040*.

Beginning in 1982 and coming to a crescendo in 1986, major philosophical changes in tax law took place. In its endless efforts to increase revenue, reduce tax rates, and close (so-called) loopholes, Congress began "phasing out" the deduction importance of Schedule A. It did this by eliminating some of the previous deductions, adding new AGI thresholds, folding in more independent forms, limiting the total deductions for taxpayers with

SCHEDULE A (1040) WRAP-UP

AGIs over $100,000, and adding more Schedule A items to the AMT (alternative minimum tax) exercise.

Congress (and the IRS), it now seems, has discovered a backhanded way of converting the deduction popularity of Schedule A into a "smoke and mirrors" scheme. The objective, of course, is to gulp more revenue into the black hole of the Federal Treasury. The result, today, is that Schedule A titled as Itemized Deductions is a deception and misnomer. The more honest title would be: *Limited Deductions*. It was in this context of limiting all individual deductions that Form 2106 was incorporated into Schedule A.

In 1986, moving expenses (Form 3903) and employee business expenses (Form 2106) each were separate (direct) offset adjustments against total income. In 1987, moving expenses were incorporated into Schedule A, and Form 2106 was formatted into two parts: Reimbursed and Unreimbursed expenses. The reimbursed expenses remained as an adjustment to income, whereas the unreimbursed expenses were incorporated into Schedule A. The Technical and Miscellaneous Revenue Act of 1988 ended the split-apart Form 2106 and mandated its total inclusion in Schedule A. Still tinkering with ways to limit deductions for employees, Congress (in 1994) drastically cut back on allowable moving-expense deductions and increased the forfeiture amount of M & E expenses (meals and entertainment) to 50% (from 20%). The political fallout was that the much less beneficial Form 3903 was reassigned *from* Schedule A back to an adjustment to income (Recall Chapter 6). Meanwhile, the Form 2106 amount on Schedule A became enmeshed in more downgrades.

As of the time of this writing, the downgrades on Schedule A affecting Form 2106 are—

1 — The 2% AGI subtraction threshold.
2 — Any net allowable deductions on Schedule A must exceed the "standard deduction" based on filing status.
3 — A 3% subtraction amount for AGIs over $100,000 applies to all Schedule A deductions.
4 — Full "add back" of all Form 2106 deductions when computing the AMT tax on Form 6251.

DEDUCTING JOB EXPENSES

As things now stand, the fate of Form 2106 proceeds as depicted in Figure 12.1. As you can see, there are four hurdles and traps representing the four downgrades listed above. We'll address each of these downgrades more specifically as we go along. First, though, we have to get you into Schedule A on the proper line.

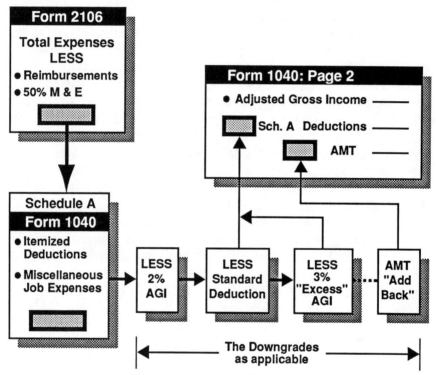

Fig. 12.1 - The "Downgrading" of Your Form 2106 Deductions

Where Form 2106 Is Entered

The preprinted instruction at the last line on Form 2106 says—

Enter the total here. Also, enter the total on Schedule A (Form 1040), line 20.

SCHEDULE A (1040) WRAP-UP

Schedule A (1996 version) is sectioned into seven different data entry blocks. The entry section, of which line 20 is the first entry, is the 6th block down. It is designated as—

Job Expenses and Most Other Miscellaneous Deductions

In other words, employee job expenses are lumped in with various other "miscellaneous" deductions. Psychologically, this does not start you off with a high priority to your Form 2106 expenses.

The line 20 of Schedule A is specifically identified as—

*Unreimbursed employee expenses — job travel, union dues, job education, etc. If required, you **MUST** attach Form 2106 or 2106-EZ.*

We already know from Chapter 10 that the last entry line on Form 2106 constitutes your net total **unreimbursed** expenses. This is because Form 2106 required you to subtract from your grand total job expenses, any reimbursements that your employer paid (NOT in Box 1 of your W-2). There is no equivocation on this matter.

The second sentence in line 20, however, reopens the dual-headed question: "Do you need to, or should you, file Form 2106 ... or Form 2106-EZ?" The instructions say—

*You MUST fill in and attach **Form 2106**, if **either** of the following applies:*

1. You claim any travel, transportation, meal, or entertainment expenses for your job, OR
2. Your employer paid you for any of your job expenses reportable on line 20.

Condition **1** is referred to as your T & E (travel and entertainment) expenses. To one degree or another, most employers reimburse their employees for their Section 162-type (trade or business) expenses; less so, for Section 212-type (occupational) expenses. If there is any reimbursement at all, Condition **2** applies. This makes a strong case for the "MUST" feature of Form 2106.

DEDUCTING JOB EXPENSES

If you are not required to file Form 2106, should you file Form 2106-EZ? As a possible clue, the instruction says—

If you used your own vehicle and [condition] *2 does not apply, you may be able to file* **Form 2106-EZ**: *Unreimbursed Employee Business Expenses, instead* [of Form 2106].

We urge using Form 2106 with attachments, even if you are not required by the MUST instructions to do so. As you'll see below, your best shot at getting through the Schedule A downsizing maze with meaningful net deductions is to use Form 2106 to its fullest.

The Lines After Form 2106

Line 20 on Schedule A (1996 version) has two dotted-line white spaces which end up as the single, solid line space: line 20. We're not sure that the IRS intended it this way, but the two dotted lines are just the right fit when there are two working spouses, each filing a separate Form 2106. If applicable, label one of the dotted lines as "H" (for husband), and one as "W" (for wife). Then hand-enter each corresponding Form 2106 amount. Sum the two and enter one total on the solid line marked "20." If there is only one Form 2106, leave the dotted lines blank. Enter the bottom line amount from Form 2106 directly onto the solid-line space at line 20.

In the same Schedule A block as line 20, there are six other entry lines. In our typical editing/abridgment manner, we portray in Figure 12.2 all of the lines in the job expenses and miscellaneous deductions block. Do note that line 24: your current year's AGI, is set off to one side. It is so, primarily as a reminder to cross-check your AGI before proceeding further.

Line 21: Tax preparation fees, is intended to require you to list these fees separately. You cannot add them in with your job expenses. The IRS uses these fees as a means of gauging the extent of any professional assistance you may have received.

Line 22: Other expenses, is restricted to those expenses directly associated with other sources of income, other than your job. Page 1 of Form 1040 lists 15 different sources of income that are tax reportable. The expenses associated with the first of these sources:

SCHEDULE A (1040) WRAP-UP

Schedule A Form 1040	JOB EXPENSES & OTHER MISCELLANY	
20	Unreimbursed employee expenses	
///	• Attach Form(s) 2106	///////
21	Tax preparation fees	
22	Other expenses. List type and amount	
23	Add lines 20 through 22 ▶	
24	Enter your AGI ▶	///////
25	Multiply line 24 by 2% (0.02) ▶	
26	Subtract line 25 from line 23	
X	Special Instructions for AGIs Over $100,000	

Fig. 12.2 - Edited Portion of Job Expenses Block on Schedule A

Wages, salaries, tips, etc. are expressly assigned to line 20. All other income-related expenses, such as investment advice, safe deposit box, custodial fees, legal fees relating to collection of income, mutual fund expenses, etc., are assigned to line 22.

Line 23 is officially identified as—

Add lines 20 through 22

This is the subtotal of all of your job and miscellaneous deductions that are subject to the 2% AGI threshold. Line 24 is your AGI. This is the amount that appears on the very last line on page 1 of Form 1040. It is labeled:

*This is your **adjusted gross income**.*

Line 25/Schedule A says—

Multiply line 24 by 2%.

This is that 2% AGI threshold that we've been telling you about. We still have more to say on this.

Line 26 officially reads—

DEDUCTING JOB EXPENSES

Subtract line 25 from line 23. If line 25 is more than line 23, enter -0- [zero].

Would we be too cynical if we were to infer from this instruction that Congress and the IRS would like nothing better than your entering "zero" at line 26? Your challenge is to justify an entry at line 26 that is well *above* zero — substantially above.

The 2% AGI Subtraction Law

In the Internal Revenue Code, the 2% AGI subtraction at line 25/Schedule A (Figure 12.2) is referred to as a "2-percent floor." Use of the word "floor" means that any amount equal to or below 2% AGI is NOT deductible, whereas any amount above it *may* be deductible. The "floor" word appears in the legislative title to Section 67, namely: ***2-Percent Floor on Miscellaneous Itemized Deductions***.

The general rule on point is subsection 67(a), namely:

In the case of an individual, the miscellaneous itemized deductions for any taxable year shall be allowed only to the extent that the aggregate of such deductions exceeds 2 percent of adjusted gross income.

There are some — not many — miscellaneous expenses that are not subject to the 2% floor. Examples are: (i) impairment-related work expenses of a disabled person; (ii) gambling losses to the extent of gambling winnings; (iii) death tax on income in respect of a decedent; and a few others.

The primary target of, and sole reason for, Section 67(a) is described in Regulation 1.67-1T(a): ***Types of expenses subject to the floor***. This regulation reads in part—

Examples of expenses that, if otherwise deductible, are subject to the 2-percent floor include, but are not limited to—

(i) Unreimbursed employee expenses, such as expenses for transportation, travel fares and lodging while away from home,

SCHEDULE A (1040) WRAP-UP

business meals and entertainment, continuing education courses, subscriptions to professional journals, union or professional dues, professional uniforms, job hunting, and the business use of the employee's home,

(ii) Expenses for the production or collection of income . . ., such as investment advisory fees, subscriptions to investment advisory publications, certain attorneys' fees, and the cost of safe deposit boxes, [and]

(iii) Expenses for the determination of any tax . . ., such as tax counsel fees and appraisal fees.

The reason for allowing deductions for expenses in excess of the percentage floor is that . . . **they constitute costs of earning income**. Elsewhere in the tax code, the cost of earning income has been an expense deduction concept of long standing. This is the principle behind Sections 162 (trade or business expenses) and 212 (occupational and investment expenses).

Anticipate/Refine Your AGI

If you want any tax beneficial job expense deductions at all, you must anticipate what each year's AGI is likely to be. Then, if you expect your unreimbursed expenses to exceed the 2% AGI floor, you should prepare yourself for all the recordkeeping associated with your claimed expenses.

Anticipation does not require an exact foreknowledge of your AGI. Approximations are good enough. For example, if your AGI is likely to be around $50,000, the percentage floor threshold that you must surpass is $1,000 (50,000 x 0.02). Correspondingly for AGIs of $100,000 and $150,000, the threshold would be $2,000 and $3,000, respectively.

In a "broad brush" approach, therefore, we suggest three expense-level criteria you might consider. These are:

    One.   If your unreimbursed expenses are not likely to exceed $1,000, chances are your deduction benefits will be nil. No records necessary.

DEDUCTING JOB EXPENSES

Two. If your expected expenses after reimbursement are between $1,000 and $2,000, the chance of any residual deductions is a toss-up. Especially if your AGI approaches $100,000.

Three. If your expected unreimbursed expenses will clearly exceed $2,000, Form 2106 is a MUST to prepare.

The 2% AGI floor is a *per taxpayer* threshold. A husband and wife filing jointly are considered to be one taxpayer. Thus, if you are married, and your spouse works, that spouse's income will increase your AGI for threshold purposes. This is why, previously, we addressed two spousal Forms 2106: one for "H", and one for "W". Even though one spouse's job expenses may not exceed the floor, it is important that that spouse prepare a Form 2106 nevertheless. The below-floor spouse's expenses help to "soak up" some of the subfloor dollars. This soaking up helps to increase the residual job-expense deductions of the above-floor spouse.

Another approach is to try to refine your AGI to be as low as possible. This means going over your income reportings on page 1 of your Form 1040 (there are 15) and your adjustments to income (there are 7) on the same page. This, at best, is a refinement process only. About the only "adjustment" that you have any discretionary control over is elective contributions to an employer-sponsored retirement plan (if any). Here, financial practicality comes into play. Thus, you reach a point where you must go forward and accept the 2% floor consequences on Schedule A.

The "Standard Deduction" Threshold

Having exceeded the 2% AGI floor for job and other miscellaneous expenses, you next face the standard deduction threshold. As you already know, all taxpayers are allowed a "standard deduction" depending on their filing status. These standards (ranging upwards from about $4,000 to nearly $7,000) are preprinted in the upper portion of page 2 of Form 1040.

The first deduction line that appears on page 2 is:

SCHEDULE A (1040) WRAP-UP

*Enter the **larger** of your:*

- *Itemized deductions from Schedule A, **OR***
- ***Standard deduction** shown below for your filing status.*

If you will glance at your Schedule A, you'll note that it consists of seven blocks of deduction entries. For review purposes here, the seven officially-titled blocks are:

1. Medical and Dental Expenses $ _____
   (subject to 7.5% AGI floor)
2. Taxes You Paid   _____
3. Interest You Paid   _____
4. Gifts to Charity   _____
5. Casualty and Theft Losses   _____
   (subject to 10% AGI floor)
6. Job Expenses and Most Other Miscellaneous Deductions (subject to 2% AGI floor)   _____
7. Other Miscellaneous Deductions   _____
   (NOT subject to the 2% floor)

One's first impulse is to total all of your "itemized" deductions, compare with the standard deduction, then go on to page 2 of Form 1040. Before you do this totaling, you'd better stop and read the official interrogation at the bottom of Schedule A.

As edited and paraphrased, you are pointedly asked:

Is your AGI over $100,000?

If you answer "No," you are told:

Your deduction is not limited. Add the amounts on the far right column. [Compare and] enter on Form 1040, line _____ the larger of this amount or your standard deduction.

As is obvious above, once your unreimbursed job and other miscellaneous expenses exceed the 2% floor, the excess is combined with all other deductions claimed on Schedule A. In

12-11

DEDUCTING JOB EXPENSES

most cases — particularly those paying mortgage interest and property taxes — exceeding the standard deduction is not a formidable task.

The 3% "Phase Out" Law

If you answer "Yes" to the over $100,000 question at the bottom of Schedule A, you are told:

Your deduction may be limited. See [instructions] *for the amount to enter.*

"What! Another limitation?" you ask yourself in alarm. "Now what are 'they' (Congress and the IRS) up to?"

Be informed of another gimmick that "they" have come up with. It is new law Section 68: ***Overall Limitation on Itemized Deductions.*** It went into effect for tax years beginning in 1991. The idea is to "phase out" up to 80% of the Schedule A deductions for wealthy taxpayers. For purposes of Section 68, a wealthy taxpayer is one whose AGI exceeds $100,000 ($50,000 if married filing separately) . . . adjusted for inflation.

Subsection (a): General Rule, states the essence of this new law:

In the case of an individual whose adjusted gross income exceeds the applicable amount, the amount of the itemized deductions otherwise applicable for the taxable year **shall be reduced by the lesser of—**

(1) 3 percent of the excess of adjusted gross income over the applicable amount, or
(2) 80 percent of the amount of the itemized deductions otherwise allowable for such taxable year.

Subsection (b) defines the "applicable amount" as $100,000 (50,000 if married filing separately), **adjusted upward for inflation**. For 1996, the AGI phase-out threshold was $117,950 (58,975 if married filing separately). The halved amount for

SCHEDULE A (1040) WRAP-UP

married spouses filing separately is intended to thwart any tax maneuvering between married individuals.

Subsection (c) excepts from the term "itemized deductions": medical expenses, investment interest expense, wagering losses, and casualty and theft losses. Why these particular items are excepted, and no others, is not clear.

Subsection (d): Coordination With Other Limitations, is very clear. It reads in full—

*This section shall be applied **after** the application of any other limitation on the allowance of **any** itemized deduction.*

The "any" itemized deduction (other than those in subsection (c)) is obviously intended to downgrade your job expense deduction still further.

Here, for example, is how Section 68(a) works out. Suppose your AGI for 1996 is $217,950 and your otherwise total deductions on Schedule A come to $20,000 (no medical, etc.). The 80% maximum phase-out amount is $16,000 (20,000 x 0.80). Your excess AGI over the applicable threshold is $100,000 (217,950 − 117,950). The 3% of this amount is $3,000. This $3,000 is the "lesser of" the two amounts specified in Subsections 68(a)(1) and (2). Therefore, you lose another $3,000 of your unreimbursed job expenses included in your Schedule A deductions.

You've got to admit it! Congress and the IRS are truly shrewd. Or, is it deceit?

An AMT "Add Back"

We are not through yet with the gimmicks that whittle down your Form 2106 deduction benefits. We have another one for you. It's the AMT (Alternative Minimum Tax) "add back." That is, you add back on another tax form, namely: **Form 6251**, the job expenses that you were finally able to claim as deductions on Schedule A. On this new form, together with other add backs, your tax is recomputed and compared with your regular tax (using Schedule A). The final tax you pay is the *higher* of the two taxes

DEDUCTING JOB EXPENSES

(regular vs. AMT). The relative and sequential roles of Schedule A and Form 6251 are schematized in Figure 12.3.

	TAX COMPUTATIONS: DEDUCTIONS, CREDITS, ETC.	
1	Adjusted gross income (AGI)	$
2	Adjusted deductions (**from Schedule A**)	< >
3	Income after deductions	
4	Your personal exemptions	< >
5	Taxable income (subtract line 4 from line 3)	
6	**Regular tax** (for your filing status)	
7	Credits (if applicable)	< >
8	**Tentative tax** (subtract line 7 from line 6)	
9	Other taxes : AMT particularly	
10	**TOTAL TAX** (add lines 8 and 9)	

Fig. 12.3 - The Sequence of Tax Computations on Page 2 of Form 1040

The alternative minimum tax (AMT) — Sections 55 through 59 — was first enacted in 1978. The ostensible goal was to recapture excessive tax savings by high income individuals. The legislative thesis was then — and still is — that there exists a "high degree of tax inequity" between wealthy taxpayers and their lower-income counterparts.

For AMT purposes, taxpayers are treated as belonging to three distinct economic groups. Each group is identified by its AMTI (AMT income) after all applicable add backs have been factored in. The three groupings are:

- Low income ----------- up to $25,000/50,000
- Upper income --------- up to $175,000
- Wealthy income ------ over $175,000

Over the years 1978 through 1996, Congress has increased the number of add backs for individuals to where it now stands at a total of 28. The definition of an "add back" is any designated tax saving, tax preference, or tax benefit that otherwise derives from the application of existing tax law. The AMT concept is a **complete**

SCHEDULE A (1040) WRAP-UP

retaxing **procedure**. This procedure — detailed in 28 lines on Form 6251 — is quite beyond the scope of our subject: Deducting Job Expenses.

We just want you to be aware that one of the first AMT add backs to Form 6251 is—

Miscellaneous itemized deductions.
Enter the amount from Schedule A.

This category includes all of your unreimbursed job expenses that exceed the 2% AGI floor, the standard deduction, and the 3% phase-out above $100,000. Apparently, the purpose of AMT is to dampen any tax-saving benefit that is deemed to be "excessive" (?).

A Cautious Prediction

Taxpayers — all of us — can never feel comfortable about what Congress (and the IRS) will do, or not do, as the years ahead unfold. In the incessant drive for greater federal revenue, only one thing is certain. Congress will continue to dicker around, searching for more ways to limit the tax-saving benefits of employee business expenses. Actually, there are not too many more restrictions that can be imposed, without repealing Sections 162 (deductions for trade or business expenses) and 212 (deductions for income-producing expenses). If these two sections are repealed, business owners, employers, and big corporations are going to howl. In the political compromise that would follow, we can envision the time when *Employee Business Expenses* could be reinstated as an adjustment to income on page 1 of Form 1040. That's where it was in 1986 and prior years.

Why do we say this?

One reason is that unreimbursed employee expenses is clearly a **cost of earning income**. It always has been and always will be. To earn income that can be regular taxed, social security taxed, medicare taxed, and AMT taxed, active business-type expenditures have to be made. Congress, the courts, and the IRS cannot defeat the natural economic law of enterprising man. If Big Government

DEDUCTING JOB EXPENSES

wants more money, it has to share in some of the income-earning pain with employees, as it does now with business owners.

It shares in this pain — albeit reluctantly — with those who report on page 1 of Form 1040:

- *Business income or loss. Attach Schedule C*
- *Capital gain or loss. Attach Schedule D*
- *Other gains or losses. Attach Form 4797*
- *Supplemental income or loss. Attach Schedule E*
- *Farm income or loss. Attach Schedule F*

All of these entries allow one's income-earning costs (expenses plus depreciation) to be deducted **before** the net income or loss is reported on Form 1040. Why shouldn't the same justification apply to employees? Recall Figure 4.1 (on page 4-4) in this regard. The Schedules C, D, E, and F, and Form 4797 items are "above the line." Why are employees singled out for "below the line" treatment?

If Congress ever comes to grips with the economic reality facing many employees these days, it would reinstate Form 2106 as an adjustment to income (on page 1, Form 1040) where it was prior to 1987. It could do so, while keeping the 2% floor intact. The 2% AGI amount could be another subtraction line on Form 2106. The same revenue goal could be accomplished without going through the charade of Schedule A.

Why are we cautiously predicting this?

Because we don't want you to give up on **Form 2106**: *Employee Business Expenses*. No matter what all else happens, legitimate business expenses will be incurred for your earning taxable income.

ABOUT THE AUTHOR

Holmes F. Crouch

Born on a small farm in southern Maryland, Holmes was graduated from the U.S. Coast Guard Academy with a Bachelor's Degree in Marine Engineering. While serving on active duty, he wrote many technical articles on maritime matters. After attaining the rank of Lieutenant Commander, he resigned to pursue a career as a nuclear engineer.

Continuing his education, he earned a Master's Degree in Nuclear Engineering from the University of California. He also authored two books on nuclear propulsion. As a result of the tax write-offs associated with writing these books, the IRS audited his returns. The IRS's handling of the audit procedure so annoyed Holmes that he undertook to become as knowledgeable as possible regarding tax procedures. He became a licensed private Tax Practitioner by passing an examination administered by the IRS. Having attained this credential, he started his own tax preparation and counseling business in 1972.

In the early years of his tax practice, he was a regular talk-show guest on San Francisco's KGO Radio responding to hundreds of phone-in tax questions from listeners. He was a much sought-after guest speaker at many business seminars and taxpayer meetings. He also provided counseling on special tax problems, such as divorce matters, property exchanges, timber harvesting, mining ventures, animal breeding, independent contractors, selling businesses, and offices-at-home. Over the past 25 years, he has prepared nearly 10,000 tax returns for individuals, estates, trusts, and small businesses (in partnership and corporate form).

During the tax season of January through April, he prepares returns in a unique manner. During a single meeting, he completes the return . . . *on the spot!* The client leaves with his return signed, sealed, and in a stamped envelope. His unique approach to preparing returns and his personal interest in his clients' tax affairs have honed his professional proficiency. His expertise extends through itemized deductions, computer-matching of income sources, capital gains and losses, business expenses and cost of goods, residential rental expenses, limited and general partnership activities, closely-held corporations, to family farms and ranches.

He remembers spending 12 straight hours completing a doctor's complex return. The next year, the doctor, having moved away, utilized a large accounting firm to prepare his return. Their accountant was so impressed by the manner in which the prior return was prepared that he recommended the doctor travel the 500 miles each year to have Holmes continue doing it.

He recalls preparing a return for an unemployed welder, for which he charged no fee. Two years later the welder came back and had his return prepared. He paid the regular fee . . . and then added a $300 tip.

During the off season, he represents clients at IRS audits and appeals. In one case a shoe salesman's audit was scheduled to last three hours. However, after examining Holmes' documentation it was concluded in 15 minutes with "no change" to his return. In another instance he went to an audit of a custom jeweler that the IRS dragged out for more than six hours. But, supported by Holmes' documentation, the client's return was accepted by the IRS with "no change."

Then there was the audit of a language translator that lasted two full days. The auditor scrutinized more than $1.25 million in gross receipts, all direct costs, and operating expenses. Even though all expensed items were documented and verified, the auditor decided that more than $23,000 of expenses ought to be listed as capital items for depreciation instead. If this had been enforced it would have resulted in a significant additional amount of tax. Holmes strongly disagreed and after many hours explanation got the amount reduced by more than 60% on behalf of his client.

He has dealt extensively with gift, death and trust tax returns. These preparations have involved him in the tax aspects of wills, estate planning, trustee duties, probate, marital and charitable bequests, gift and death exemptions, and property titling.

Although not an attorney, he prepares Petitions to the U.S. Tax Court for clients. He details the IRS errors and taxpayer facts by citing pertinent sections of tax law and regulations. In a recent case involving an attorney's ex-spouse, the IRS asserted a tax deficiency of $155,000. On behalf of his client, he petitioned the Tax Court and within six months the IRS conceded the case.

Over the years, Holmes has observed that the IRS is not the industrious, impartial, and competent federal agency that its official public imaging would have us believe.

He found that, at times, under the slightest pretext, the IRS has interpreted against a taxpayer in order to assess maximum penalties, and may even delay pending matters so as to increase interest due on additional taxes. He has confronted the IRS in his own behalf on five separate occasions, going before the U.S. Claims Court, U.S. District Court, and U.S. Tax Court. These were court actions that tested specific sections of the Internal Revenue Code which he found ambiguous, inequitable, and abusively interpreted by the IRS.

Disturbed by the conduct of the IRS and by the general lack of tax knowledge by most individuals, he began an innovative series of taxpayer-oriented Federal tax guides. To fulfill this need, he undertook the writing of a series of guidebooks that provide in-depth knowledge on one tax subject at a time. He focuses on subjects that plague taxpayers all throughout the year. Hence, his formulation of the "Allyear" Tax Guide series.

The author is indebted to his wife, Irma Jean, and daughter, Barbara MacRae, for the word processing and computer graphics that turn his experiences into the reality of these publications. Holmes welcomes comments, questions, and suggestions from his readers. He can be contacted in California at (408) 867-2628, or by writing to the publisher's address.

ALLYEAR Tax Guides
by Holmes F. Crouch

Series 100 - INDIVIDUALS AND FAMILIES

BEING SELF-EMPLOYED .... T/G 101
DEDUCTING JOB EXPENSES .... T/G 102
RESOLVING DIVORCE ISSUES .... T/G 104
CITIZENS WORKING ABROAD .... T/G 105

Series 200 - INVESTORS AND BUSINESSES

INVESTOR GAINS & LOSSES .... T/G 201
HOBBY BUSINESS VENTURES .... T/G 202
STARTING YOUR BUSINESS .... T/G 203
MAKING PARTNERSHIPS WORK .... T/G 204

Series 300 - RETIREES AND ESTATES

DECISIONS WHEN RETIRING .... T/G 301
WRITING YOUR WILL .... T/G 302
SIMPLIFYING YOUR ESTATE .... T/G 303
YOUR EXECUTOR DUTIES .... T/G 304
YOUR TRUSTEE DUTIES .... T/G 305

Series 400 - OWNERS AND SELLERS

RENTAL REAL ESTATE .... T/G 401
OWNING NATURAL RESOURCES .... T/G 402
SELLING YOUR HOME .... T/G 404
SELLING YOUR BUSINESS .... T/G 405

Series 500 - AUDITS AND APPEALS

KEEPING GOOD RECORDS .... T/G 501
WINNING YOUR AUDIT .... T/G 502
DISAGREEING WITH THE IRS .... T/G 503
GOING INTO TAX COURT .... T/G 505

All of the above available at bookstores, libraries, and on the internet

For a free 8-page catalog,
or information about the above titles, contact:
ALLYEAR Tax Guides
20484 Glen Brae Drive, Saratoga, CA 95070
Phone: (408) 867-2628   Fax: (408) 867-6466